SIX ARCHITECTS

Copyright © 2017 Read Books Ltd.
This book is copyright and may not be
reproduced or copied in any way without
the express permission of the publisher in writing

British Library Cataloguing-in-Publication Data
A catalogue record for this book is available from the
British Library

Architecture

Architecture (from the Latin *architectura*, after the Greek *arkhitekton*, meaning chief builder) is both the process and the product of planning, designing, and constructing buildings and other physical structures. It is an incredibly important part of human existence – starting from the simplest aspects of survival, yet also functioning as a cultural symbol, a works of art, and as a means of identification of past civilisations.

Building first evolved out of the dynamics between needs (shelter, security, worship, etc.) and means (available building materials and attendant skills). As human cultures developed and knowledge began to be formalized through oral traditions and practices, building became a craft, and 'architecture' was the formalised version of this craft. In many ancient civilizations, such as those of Egypt and Mesopotamia, architecture and urbanism reflected the constant engagement with the divine and the supernatural. Many ancient cultures resorted to monumentality in architecture (think of the Pyramids at Giza, or the Parthenon at Athens) to represent symbolically the political power of the ruler, the ruling elite, or the state itself.

The architecture and urbanism of the Classical civilizations such as the Greeks and the Romans generally evolved from civic ideals rather than religious or empirical ones – and new building types emerged. Architectural 'style' developed in the form of the Classical orders. The earliest surviving written work on the subject of architecture is *De Architectura*, by the Roman architect Vitruvius in the early first-century CE. According to Vitruvius, a good building should satisfy the three principles of *firmitas, utilitas,* and *venustas,* translating as 'durability', 'utility' and 'beauty'.

Early Asian writings on architecture include the *Kao Gong Ji* of China from the seventh century BCE; the *Shilpa Shastras* of ancient India and the *Manjusri Vasthu Vidya Sastra* of Sri Lanka. The architecture of different parts of Asia developed along different lines from that of Europe; Buddhist, Hindu and Sikh architecture each having different characteristics. Islamic architecture began in the seventh century CE, incorporating architectural forms from the ancient Middle East and Byzantium, but also developing features to suit the religious and social needs of the society. In Europe during the Medieval period, guilds were formed by craftsmen to organize their trades and written contracts have survived, particularly in relation to ecclesiastical buildings. From about 900 CE onwards, the movements of both clerics and tradesmen carried architectural knowledge across Europe, resulting in the pan-European styles Romanesque and Gothic.

In Renaissance Europe, from about 1400 onwards, there was a revival of Classical learning accompanied by the development of Renaissance Humanism, which placed greater emphasis on the role of the individual in society. Buildings were ascribed to specific architects – Brunelleschi, Alberti, Michelangelo, Palladio – and the cult of the individual had begun. Leone Battista Alberti, who elaborates on the ideas of Vitruvius in his treatise, *De Re Aedificatoria*, saw beauty primarily as a matter of proportion, although ornament also played a part. For Alberti, the rules of proportion were those that governed the idealised human figure; 'the Golden mean'.

The notion of 'style' in the arts was not developed until the sixteenth century, with the writing of Vasari. By the eighteenth century, his *Lives of the Most Excellent Painters, Sculptors, and Architects* had been translated into Italian, French, Spanish and English. With the emerging knowledge in scientific fields and the rise of new materials and technology, architecture and engineering further began to separate, and the architect began to concentrate on aesthetics and the humanist aspects, often at the expense of technical aspects of building design. Around this time, there was also the rise of the 'gentleman architect' who usually concentrated on visual qualities derived from historical prototypes, typified by the many country houses of Great Britain that were created in the Neo Gothic or Scottish Baronial styles.

The nineteenth-century English art critic, John Ruskin, in his *Seven Lamps of Architecture* (published 1849), had a representative view of what constituted architecture. Architecture was the 'art which so disposes and adorns the edifices raised by men ... that the sight of them contributes to his mental health, power, and pleasure.' For Ruskin, the aesthetic was of overriding significance. His work goes on to state that a building is not truly a work of architecture unless it is in some way 'adorned'. Around the beginning of the twentieth century, a general dissatisfaction with the emphasis on revivalist architecture and elaborate decoration gave rise to many new lines of thought that served as precursors to Modern Architecture.

Notable among these schools is the *Deutscher Werkbund*, formed in 1907 to produce better quality machine made objects. Following this lead, the *Bauhaus school*, founded in Weimar in 1919, redefined the architectural bounds; viewing the creation of a building as the ultimate synthesis – the apex of art, craft, and technology. When Modern architecture was first practiced, it was an avant-garde movement with moral, philosophical, and aesthetic underpinnings. Immediately after World War I, pioneering modernist architects sought to develop a completely new style appropriate for a new post-war social and economic order, focused on meeting the needs of the middle and working classes.

On the difference between the ideals of architecture and mere construction, the renowned twentieth-century architect Le Corbusier wrote:

> You employ stone, wood, and concrete, and with these materials you build houses and palaces: that is construction. Ingenuity is at work. But suddenly you touch my heart, you do me good. I am happy and I say: This is beautiful. That is Architecture.

Architecture itself has an incredibly long and fascinating history. As long as humans have been around, we have needed places to live, and have sought ways to make these spaces beautiful and functional. As our societies continue to change, so does the architecture which reflects them. It is hoped that the current reader enjoys this book on the subject.

SIX ARCHITECTS

BY

SIR REGINALD BLOMFIELD, R.A.
M.A., HON. LITT.D., F.S.A., P.P.R.I.B.A.

HON. FELLOW OF EXETER COLLEGE, OXFORD, AND HON. MEMBER OF
THE ROYAL ACADEMY OF BELGIUM AND OF THE ACADEMY OF ARTS
AND LETTERS AND THE NATIONAL ACADEMY OF DESIGN OF AMERICA

PREFACE

THIS volume contains the substance of Lectures delivered at the University College of Wales, Aberystwyth, on the Aberystwyth Lectures Foundation during the Session 1934–35. In them I have made no attempt to give an exhaustive account of the subjects of my study. Indeed, in the case of two at least of them, Inigo Jones and François Mansart, the actual materials are very scanty, and in no case have I approached the subject from a technical point of view. My aim has been, so far as possible, to disentangle the personality of each of these famous Architects, and to present some idea of the sort of men they actually were, so far as one can form any opinion from their work and the records that exist. The art of Architecture is as personal and intimate as that of the Painter and Sculptor, a fact that is too often lost sight of in the zeal for classification of the Art by styles and periods, and it is to this human side that I have addressed myself. It is perhaps too much to hope that these critical studies will induce the younger generation to study the masterpieces of a bygone art. A list of Authorities is given at the end of this volume.

HAMPSTEAD, 1935

CONTENTS

	PAGE
ANDREA PALLADIO	1
LORENZO BERNINI	33
INIGO JONES	67
JACQUES FRANÇOIS MANSART	101
ANGE JACQUES GABRIEL	129
CHRISTOPHER WREN	157
INDEX	191

ILLUSTRATIONS

	FACE PAGE
ANDREA PALLADIO	2
GIOVANNI LORENZO BERNINI	34
INIGO JONES	68
FRANÇOIS MANSART	102
ANGE JACQUES GABRIEL	130
SIR CHRISTOPHER WREN	158

ANDREA PALLADIO

ANDREA PALLADIO
From a portrait by Paolo Veronese. Engraved by Picart, 1716, for Leone's edition of Palladio

ANDREA PALLADIO

It is the fashion just now to ignore the past and to regard it with contempt, without any serious attempt to ascertain what the past does and must always mean for the present. I am therefore going to fly in the face of this fashion, and talk to you of six famous architects, two Italian, two French and two English, men who are in danger of being forgotten by the younger generation. Yet all of them were men who left their ineffaceable mark on architecture and have got to be considered whether one likes their work or not. It is one of the most mischievous mistakes of inverted Modernism that it is possible to wipe out the past and begin again with a clean slate. "Tabulae novae" has always been the cry of the bankrupt and the revolutionary. Down with everything, and then we can begin all over again, do just what we like and, let me add, create the worst of all possible tyrannies, the tyranny of ignorance. However, in these studies I am not going to concern myself with revolutionists.

I have given my views elsewhere on the wrong sort of modernism, and in spite of the suggestion of one of my critics that anyone who refuses to accept the fashions of the day is like Mrs Partington trying to keep out the Atlantic with a mop, I see no reason either in the art and literature of the day, or in the history of the past, to induce me to abandon my position. On the contrary, I even hope that the reflections which I may offer on the subjects of these studies may lead some of our modernists to think that after all there *is* something to be learnt from the past that may be of use to us in the present, and may enable us to face the uncertainties of the future with reasonable confidence. I wish to make quite clear the standpoint from which I approach my subject. I wholly dissent from the Bolshevism now rampant in the arts, that disease which I have called elsewhere "Modernismus", which offers weird geometrical diagrams, empty picture frames, disgusting nightmares and worse, as the last word of painting, shapeless lumps or negroid horrors as sculpture, packing-cases with holes at regular intervals as architecture, unpleasant noises as music and gibberish as literature. The whole of this false modernism is based on the assumption that the past can be treated as non-existent, and that people can start "de novo", as if they had been dropped on to the earth out of space from some unknown and unknowable planet. But we are the children of the past as well as people living in the present, children of those who have gone before us in this world, and we cannot disown our heritage even if we are foolish enough to try, because that heritage is not something separate and isolated that can be taken or left, but is an actual part of ourselves, ingrained in us beyond the possibility of detachment, however much we may try to shake it off. George Edmund Street, the strong man of the Gothic revivalists, placed on the title-page of one of his books the text, "The old ways which are the better". If this is taken literally it is all wrong, for the fact that the ways are old is neither here nor there, and it is the spirit not the letter that is vital. But I am all for the right understanding and use of tradition, and that is something very different from the literal reproduction of old work as practised by the revivalists almost down to the late war. I want to be quite clear on this point, for I have been much misrepresented. Traditionalism as I understand it is a wholly different thing from revivalism. Some of my young modernist critics have tried to tie me down to the advocacy of a slavish use of details of the past, the orders of architecture for example, but I have never been guilty of that folly. To me these details are no more than the words of the language, a vocabulary which may or may not be used as one pleases. There is as much room for artistry in the way they are used as there is in the skilful use of quite familiar words in literature. What I understand by traditionalism is not a matter of detail at all, but the sense of continuousness, the will to regard oneself as a link in the chain that connects the past and present with the future. It is in fact the same thing as modernism if that is rightly understood, for true modernism is the right and inevitable advance of civilization on lines proved by the accumulated experience of the past. It takes account of changing needs, of increased knowledge and wider outlook, and of the new problems that present themselves with each generation. It sets out to meet those problems, equipped with the knowledge of the past as well as of the present, and it carries forward a road that started far back in the first beginnings of civilization. It is traditionalist in the sense that it realizes the extent and value of its inheritance, but it is not hide-bound by tradition. It moves on with the full freedom of knowledge. The assumption that we are psychologically quite different from our fathers has no foundation. Let me quote a passage from the *Religio Medici* of Sir Thomas Browne: "Opinions do find after certain revolutions, men and minds like those who first begat them. To see ourselves again we need not look for Plato's year.[1] Every man is not only himself . . . men are lived over again, the world is now as it was in ages past. There was none then, but there hath been someone since that parallels him, and [is] as it were his revived self." I commend this saying of the wise old physician of Norwich to the meditations of the young men of "Modernismus". And let me add another saying from that sagacious if unattractive person, Francis Bacon: "It were good that men in their innovations should follow the example of time itself, which indeed innovates greatly, but quietly and by degrees scarce to be perceived". It is from this point of view that I approach my subject, and the text I would

[1] "Plato's year" was one that would repeat itself every thousand years.

take for my title is one that is quite out of fashion: "Let us now praise famous men". Let us see if something may not yet be learnt from those who have gone before us.

I shall begin with a famous Italian of the sixteenth century, Andrea Palladio, an architect now entirely out of fashion, and little more than a name to our architectural students. Yet Palladio was the most famous architect of his time, not only in Italy but Western Europe, and for the first fifty years of the eighteenth century was regarded in England as the admirable and unexceptionable model of architecture. Little is really known of his life. Leoni, the Venetian architect, who came to England early in the eighteenth century and produced a fine English version of Palladio's "Four Books" in 1715, only knew that "he flourished in the sixteenth century and died in 1580". Palladio was born at Vicenza in 1518 and was the son of Pietro, a stone-mason of that city. He is said to have begun as a sculptor, probably helping his father, for stone-masons in Italy in the sixteenth century meant a good deal more than the monumental mason of our day, and the term should be understood to mean a worker in stone, an artist who could carve the friezes, arabesques, capitals, modillions and all the interminable details in which all but the best of the architects of the Renaissance delighted. It seems that Andrea Palladio must have given up this work and devoted himself to the study of architecture at an early date, and if an entry of a payment to "Messer Andrea architetto" in 1541 refers to Andrea Palladio, he must have been recognized as an architect at the age of twenty-two, and must have been important enough to have his portrait painted not very long afterwards by a certain Bernardino Licinio, a relation of Pordenone. How Palladio obtained his training is not known, but he seems to have shown unusual ability and intelligence as a boy, and is said to have begun his study of architecture before he was fourteen while in the service of Gian Giorgio Trissino, a wealthy and important person in Vicenza, a poet and an enthusiastic amateur of architecture. Trissino thought so highly of the boy that he took him to Rome in 1541 to study the remains of classical architecture, and either on this occasion or later he visited Ancona, Rimini, Naples and Capua. It is unfortunate that he never went on from Naples to Paestum, for not a single Italian architect right down to the latter part of the eighteenth century seems to have been aware that Italy possessed in the Temple of Neptune at Paestum one of the finest examples of Greek architecture in existence. In 1547 he was at Tivoli, and he is said to have been summoned to Rome in 1549 by Paul III to advise on the completion of S. Peter's. The Pope died before he reached Rome and the whole story seems to be very doubtful. Palladio was again at Rome in 1551 in the company of certain Venetian gentlemen, and he published the results of his labours, *La Antichita di Roma* at Rome in 1554. Though Palladio was by no means first in the field in the study of the antiquities of Rome, his drawings were a good deal in advance of those of his predecessors. In the preface to the fourth Book of his Architecture he says that all the details that he gives were made from measurements taken by himself on the spot. That he did a great deal of careful work there can be no doubt, but he was inaccurate, and was not endowed with any scrupulous sense of scholarship, and the connoisseurs were very easily satisfied. It was not in fact till the reign of Louis XIV that the remains of the great buildings of Imperial Rome were accurately drawn and measured by Desgodetz.

Palladio's first important work was the casing in of the Sala della Ragione at Vicenza, in 1549. The problem here was to case in a vast Gothic hall, and Palladio erected a two-storey arcade with columns, balustrades and entablatures, a Doric order below and an Ionic above, all according to the rules of antiquity as he understood them from his study of Vitruvius and the buildings of Ancient Rome. He paid not the slightest regard to the character of the existing building, and did all he could to disguise its purpose and bury its individuality. In spite of its technical accomplishment I do not admire this building very much; it is all so elaborate and artificial, a characteristic example of the Italian weakness for façades, concealing something very different behind an imposing front. Palladio seems to have regarded it as his finest work, but artists are not always the best judges of their own achievements, and Palladio was to do very much better than this in his churches at Venice, in his country houses on the Brenta and indeed in one instance at Vicenza itself. The great fragment of the Casa del Diavolo, two bays only of what was to have been a composition of seven bays, shows what Palladio could do when he could shake himself free of unnecessary detail and his own erudition. His palaces at Vicenza finished in stucco made a great sensation at the time, and were fully illustrated by Palladio himself. He seems to have been forced to make bricks without straw. He had to make an imposing parade with scanty resources, and he followed the Italian instinct for gesture and display, its passion for theatrical magnificence, provided it did not cost too much. So Palladio built his palaces of brick and covered them with stucco ornament, instead of searching for the intrinsic artistic value of brick itself, such as Peruzzi had found in his great palace at Bologna. The most attractive of his palaces at Vicenza is the Palazzo Chierigati, with its open loggias on the ground and first floors, and its excellent proportions. Palladio was not responsible for those silly urns and figures above the main cornice. In the figure in his second Book they don't exist, much to the advantage of the design—the weak point of the design is the single columns and arch with no abutment at the external angles, and if Palladio's reputation had rested only on his work at Vicenza I think it might have gone the way of many of his palaces. In this regard he was the victim of his clients, persons of importance in a provincial town, anxious to figure as magnificent patrons of the arts. The famous theatre of Vicenza is a characteristic example of the fashion of the time. The Virtuosi decided that they must have a theatre at Vicenza in the antique manner, so Palladio set to work and designed his very ingenious theatre on what was supposed to be the lines of a Greek theatre, to which it bears not the very slightest resemblance. His triumphal arch at Vicenza is rather thin in design, and Palladio's title to rank among the immortals cannot rest on these rather doubtful foundations. One must look elsewhere, and we shall find ourselves on firmer ground in those admirable churches of S. Georgio and Il Redentore (1576) in Venice, and in those attractive "villas", really small country houses, that he built in the neighbourhood of Vicenza and along the banks of the Brenta between Padua and Venice. These are fully described and illustrated in the second of Palladio's Books, for it has to be admitted that though Palladio's enthusiasm for the antique was genuine enough, the success of Andrea Palladio was not to be forgotten, and one whole book of his four Books on architecture is devoted to the illustration and advertisement of designs by the author himself. Yet his villas are admirable in their way, and on quite a different footing from the pretentious palaces of Vicenza, for as a rule they are treated very simply, and their interiors, such as that of the Villa Malcontenta on the banks of the Brenta a few miles from Venice, are designed with an austere reticence which is singularly attractive. The Villa Capra or Almerigo, known as the Rotonda, built from Palladio's designs for the Referendary Paolo Almerigo, was so much admired in the eighteenth century that it was reproduced "totidem verbis" at Footscray and Mereworth in Kent, and was regarded by the Cognoscenti of the eighteenth century much as the Petit Trianon has since been regarded in French architecture. The Villa Capra is in its way a masterpiece of monumental design. It is just a square block with a shallow dome over the centre and projecting porticoes with wide flights of steps on all four sides, but its beautiful proportions, the fine reticence of its detail, and the rhythm that governs every part of the design of the exterior, make it the best thing of its kind ever done. It is a standing example of what may be done with simple means when guided by great knowledge and fastidious taste, in absolute contrast to the arid and ignorant design which under the guise of "efficiency" and "functionalism" makes the architectural efforts of the Modernismist so hopelessly unattractive. Palladio's villas are in some ways his most original and characteristic work. He here struck out a completely new line in domestic architecture. His fine sense of proportion had free play in these relatively modest country houses, and he did not have to contend with the combined vanity and impecuniosity of his clients, as had been his fate at Vicenza. My impression is that he did not really find himself till he moved into the spacious atmosphere of Venice. At the end of the sixteenth century, Venice seems to me to have been about the one place in Italy in which the air, moral and political, was not more or less malignant. The rulers of the Republic with all their faults were men of large ideas and resolute character, and here Palladio was not to be stinted in money or made to do foolish things. Here he was given stone and marble instead of paint and stucco, and he now found his real self, and showed what he could do in the churches of San Georgio and Il Redentore, the latter one of the finest interiors of a church of moderate size ever built. The church was begun by the Republic in 1576 to commemorate the passing of a Plague. Palladio, who died four years later, hardly saw its completion. It was his latest work and sums up all that was best in his architecture. It was his last word, the fitting conclusion of a great career. It was also the last word of the sixteenth century, for Bernini and Borromini were to follow, and the ideals that Palladio had sought to establish in his four Books of architecture, were to be lost in the unbridled licence of the Baroque.

I have already called attention to Palladio's researches into the antiquities of Rome, published in 1554, and some sixteen years later he returned to his old love and issued in 1570 his famous four Books on architecture, a work which more than any of his buildings has preserved his reputation to this day when abler architects are forgotten. "Littera scripta manet". The architect who writes, if he writes to any purpose, has a mean advantage over his fellows, because people read his books who never see their buildings, and Palladio's work was accepted as a sort of gospel of architecture second only to Vitruvius. It professed to give an accurate presentation of the details of classical, that is,

Roman architecture, for unfortunately these men knew nothing of Greek, and it described and classified the buildings of antiquity with examples from the ruins of Rome and illustrations from his own work. It was undoubtedly an able, if inaccurate, work, which brought the neo-classic architecture of the Renaissance up to date and became, as Palladio had intended, the text-book of architecture. In his dedication to Count Giacomo Angaranno, Palladio claimed that not only had he given years of study to the art of architecture, but that he had visited, seen with his own eyes and measured with his own hands the remains of Antiquity in Rome and in other places not only in Italy but elsewhere. He refers to the famous staircase at Chambord, though it is doubtful if he had ever seen it, and gives details of the Maison Carrée and the Temple of Nemausus at Nîmes, but with this exception he does not appear to have travelled far outside Italy, and in Italy he confined his researches to Rome and its neighbourhood and never went to Paestum or Sicily. His book begins in the approved manner of Vitruvius with some notes on building materials and foundations, but these are soon over, and Palladio devotes himself to his main subject, a detailed account of the orders of architecture which completes his first book, and leads on to the second book which describes buildings designed by himself, and the application of antiquity to modern practice. The third book deals with Bridges, Piazzas, the Palaestras and Basilicas of the Ancients, not omitting an account and illustrations of Palladio's design of the "Basilica" at Vicenza. This book was dedicated to a new patron, Emanuel Philibert, Duke of Savoy. The fourth book deals with ancient temples in Rome and elsewhere, including illustrations of a Temple at Pola, the Maison Carrée, very fully illustrated, and that remarkable fragment, the Temple of Nemausus in the Jardin de la Fontaine at Nîmes.

What was the value of Palladio's four Books on architecture? The habit of producing books on architecture with illustrations from works designed by the architect himself was already established. De l'Orme had done this in his immense book on architecture, and with the practical instinct of the Frenchman had devoted much of it to building construction, with his own personal observations and notes. The aim of Palladio's book was different. It was addressed not to architects and builders, but to Virtuosi with a fashionable interest in architecture. It was undoubtedly the result of much research, but Palladio was by no means the first in the field. Alberti had written his ten books, *De Re Ædificatoria* more than one hundred years before Palladio. That rather mysterious scholar and architect, Fra Giocondo, wrote a commentary on Vitruvius which was published at Florence in 1513. Sebastian Serlio published the first of his books on architecture in 1532 and completed the series in 1540. Marliani's "Urbis Romæ Topographiae" dedicated to Francis I, appeared in 1535, and went through eleven editions in the sixteenth century. Pyrrho Ligori's Antiquities of Rome was published at Venice in 1553. Albertini, Pomponius Leto, Fulvio, Fauno, Labacco and others had all dealt with the Antiquities of Rome before Palladio, and Etienne Du Perac of Paris published his valuable perspective views of the ruins of Rome in 1575. The learned edition of Vitruvius by Daniele Barbaro, Patriarch of Aquileia, was published at Venice in 1567, and it is evident from the pocket editions of works on Architecture published in Italy in the sixteenth century, such as the Venetian edition of Alberti, 1546, and the very rare edition of Fra Giocondo's Vitruvius, published at Florence in 1513, that a keen interest was being taken in architecture and a good deal known about it long before Palladio wrote his four Books. In actual fact Palladio's scholarship was of a somewhat superficial order. The measurements that he gives of old buildings are not to be trusted. Serlio had covered the same ground with greater accuracy and honesty, but Serlio was a modest man with no capacity for self-advertisement, and his career ended in obscurity and bitter disappointment among the adventurers at the Court of Francis I. Palladio, a far more astute person, probably realized that there was nobody capable of challenging his pronouncements, and he gratified the taste of the time, and what a modern critic calls "the finality complex", by restorations of the buildings that he illustrated. The real interest of Palladio's four Books lies in the one which he devoted to the illustration of his own works, and I have an uncomfortable suspicion that personal advertisement was not an unimportant motive for the work, and, that Palladio yielded to that anxiety for "réclame" which has too often prevented Architecture from taking the rank which it claims as one of the learned professions. Yet when one has discounted personal motives, superficial scholarship and inaccuracies, Palladio's *Architectura* is a remarkable work; it is clearly arranged, admirably illustrated. It met, more than any other book yet published, the want felt at the time for a definite formulation of architecture, a text-book to which all could appeal, and though the French preferred Vignola's account of the orders, Palladio's Architecture continued to be the standard work till swept away by the Romantic movement.

You may be surprised that in selecting Palladio for one of my subjects I have made no attempt to present him as an immaculate hero. My view of the duty of a historical critic is that he should collect the evidence available, present it as he sees it, and leave it to others to test his views by their own observations, so I ask where are we to place Palladio in our gallery of famous men?

In the Museo Civico at Vicenza, there is a photograph of a portrait medallion of Palladio, showing the features of a man of thirty, almost Greek in their refinement and serenity, and on a bracket above is a bust of

Palladio, which presents him as an elderly, careworn man, with a sharp nose and ill-shaped head, who appears to be making a strenuous effort to look intellectual. Then there is the portrait which forms the frontispiece of Leoni's edition of Palladio, attributed to no less a person than Paolo Caliari il Veronese, which suggests a morose, rather truculent person, not at all the austere scholar or the suave professional architect. Which is right? The medallion, the bust, or the picture? Was Palladio a scholar, a sincere artist, a master of abstract form, was he only a more or less meritorious pedant, or was he just an ambitious thruster? I do not think that any of these descriptions meet the case completely, because to some extent elements of all three were present, and as one sometimes finds with other men of great ability, there was just a strain of the mountebank in his affectation of profound scholarship. Yet when all is said, Palladio was a great architect, and his work remains a landmark in the development of architecture, the swan-song as it were of a movement that had begun with Alberti, but was now to be lost in Italy and the countries within its immediate range of influence. For Palladio was forgotten on the

Continent soon after his death. It was only in England that his reputation lasted, introduced by Inigo Jones in the reign of Charles I, lost in the civil war, and only revived in the eighteenth century by amateurs such as Lord Burlington and those rather obsequious architects such as Colen Campbell and Kent who ignored the genial manner of Wren, and designed vast country houses in the strict Palladian manner.

Palladio was in fact the last representative of a great tradition. In the preface to his "Architecture" he refers to Giacomo Sansovino as having first introduced the true manner of design, but the line of successors, of which he himself was the last, goes much further back. Brunelleschi died in 1446, Alberti, that prince among architects, who wrote ten books on architecture, died in 1472, Bramante in 1514, Fra Giocondo in 1515 and Giuliano da San Gallo in 1516, Raphael in 1520 and Sansovino in 1529. Thus ten years before Palladio was born, neo-classic architecture had firmly established itself in Italy and had reached a splendid height of technical attainment based on the ruins of Rome, but varied according to the personalities of these men of genius. Their tradition was carried on by the younger generation of their contemporaries, Antonio da San Gallo the elder, who died in 1534, Baldassare Peruzzi, perhaps the most original and the finest architect of all these brilliant men, who died in 1536, Antonio da San Gallo the younger who died in 1546, Sanmichele, who died in 1559, and, last of all, Michael Angelo, 1564, the glorious rebel who was to be bound by no formula, and followed the bidding of his own tremendous genius. Palladio is hardly to be ranked with any of these men; he ranks rather with Vignola, his contemporary and rival, who died in 1573. When Palladio began serious practice, a little before the middle of the sixteenth century, he might have taken any one of these architects as his model, but they had all gone their several ways, there was no definite school, and it was here that Palladio came in, and made it his business to formulate and if possible stabilize a manner of architecture that was already showing signs of breaking up. His four Books appeared at the exact psychological moment. Somebody was wanted to sum up the result of the work of the last hundred years. The great effort of the Renaissance was over. That whirlwind of energy and enthusiasm which had swept through every nook and cranny of the Arts, was spent, the reaction was setting in, and of that reaction Palladio was the nice exponent. More orderly in his method than Serlio, more comprehensive than Vignola, with the touch of pedantry that gave his writings a fallacious air of scholarship, he was the very man to summarize, classify and formulate a system. After the giants came the schoolmaster to put everything in order.

Yet that again is not the whole story, for apart from his written work, there remains his actual architecture to be taken into account, and in estimating this it is right to consider the conditions under which he worked, first at Vicenza, then in the period of the villas, and finally in Venice, and we shall find that his art was steadily advancing as he won wider freedom and was given greater opportunity. Too much importance should not be attached to his stucco palaces, and the fantastic experiment of the theatre at Vicenza. Palladio had, or thought he had, to please his clients, and these included Counts and Marquises and others who wanted a great display at little cost. Society at Vicenza in the sixteenth century would have made an interesting psychological study. Comparatively speaking, Vicenza was a small provincial town which had played no particular part in history. Mantegna was born there but he worked elsewhere. The leaders of society at Vicenza were no doubt anxious to persuade themselves and others that they were really among the great men of the earth, so they began with stone and brick, went on with stucco, and left the back of their buildings anyhow.

Palladio had little sense of material. Probably because he had to economise, he was very sparing in his use of stone and he never realized the possibilities of simple brick, or of brick in combination with stone as Wren used it at Hampton Court. Nor did he appreciate the use of a plain wall as Peruzzi had used it on the Palazzo Albergati at Bologna. With all its undeniable merits, Palladio's architecture was essentially Academic and, if I may so put it, shows little sense of humour, or perhaps one should say he felt himself rigorously bound by his own conventions, and by a conscientious anxiety to satisfy the foolish demands of his patrons, the Cognoscenti of Vicenza. When he got away from Vicenza, Palladio seems to have shaken off this baleful influence, and in the larger atmosphere of Venice he showed himself capable of relying for his effect on those time-honoured and now forgotten elements of fine architectural design, scale, proportion, mass, silhouette, that "ordonnance" which means and requires the habit of thinking in big terms. He had shaken off all that tedious and interminable ornament that used to be considered the hallmark of Renaissance architecture and was in fact its most deplorable feature. In the interiors of some of his villas, and more particularly in the two churches at Venice, there is an attractive sense of spaciousness, and one can enjoy in these buildings an abstract beauty of form, and an equable coolness of design which acquires a high value in comparison with the turbulence of later Italian work.

Palladio died in the year 1580 full of honour. Temanza, his biographer, describes him as a rather small man, of a good presence and genial countenance (which does not agree with his portraits), witty and of good address, who kept on excellent terms with the great people whom he met in the course of his profession, altogether an attractive person, not the pedant one might suppose from his writings, or the truculent villain suggested by his engraved portrait. He was a member of the Academy of Florence, and numbered among his friends Paolo Veronese, Federigo Zucchero, Vasari, Jacopo Sansovino, and Pietro Cataneo, the architect. He was an excellent draughtsman, and of all the designs for the completion of San Petronio at Bologna kept in the Sacristy, his is much the best so far as draughtsmanship goes, and the collection includes designs by such men as Peruzzi, Giulio Romano, Vignola, Terribilia, and others. He made all the drawings for his own books, and is said to have made those given in Barbaro's Vitruvius. Vasari, who had a very high opinion of Palladio, called him "Architetto Chiarissimo". Somebody else called him the "Titian of Architects", a singularly inept description, for Palladio's invention, whatever his merits, showed no trace of the glorious opulence of Titian. Algarotti was a little happier with his "Raphael of Architects". The authorities at Venice thought so highly of him that after his death they recorded his name in the churches of San Giorgio and Santa Lucia.

Our Modernismists probably regard Palladio and his work as gone beyond redemption. Yet he still deserves close study, if only for the understanding of the architecture of the last three hundred years, and to teach students that there is such a thing as a standard in architectural design, and one that they do well to observe until they are able to walk by themselves. I find that in an essay on Palladio, which was published nearly thirty years ago, I said that I had ventured some criticisms on his work, "because in the erratic, I might say, chaotic, state of modern architectural taste, there is a danger of a too abrupt revulsion from anarchy to rigid dogmatism in design and the restoration of Palladio as an object of idol worship. To talk about him as 'our master' and the like, only leads to pedantry and dulness. In the present state of uncertainty the study of architecture is extremely important, and it is essential that careful critical study should be applied to the architecture of the past, and that the facts should be presented in true historical perspective and proportion."

These words sound strange to us nowadays when the study of the past is extinct, and everybody goes as he pleases, but I adhere to every word of this. What surprises me now is that thirty years ago the advanced young men of the schools were making a fetish of Palladio.

Now, I doubt if their successors have heard of him, for the cry is for the immediate present and damn the past and all its ways and works. But real progress does not lie this way. Our young men must retrace their steps and return to the high road, if their work is to have any lasting value. They must shake themselves free of "la folle ambition de se singulariser et de passer pour créateurs ou réformateurs de l'architecture", an ambition for which Palladio, as one of his biographers says, had the profoundest contempt. It was the stand which Palladio made against this tendency which was the essential service that he rendered to architecture. The position he occupies in the development of Italian architecture is not unlike that of Chambers the English architect in the eighteenth century. Both men were purists, and their high professional ability was not endangered by too many of those "brilliant flashes of genius" which are supposed to rise out of space and justify any aberration of design. Both men made a deliberate stand against the fashionable licence of their time, and did what they could to recall the art of architecture to the graver practice of the past. It is a service that more than ever wants doing again to-day. The work of steadying English architecture, of rescuing it from the quagmire of "Modernismus" has yet to be done, if it is to resume its rightful place in the living procession of history. So in spite of his essentially academic mind and his obsession by precedent, I still recommend Palladio to the attention of our young architects. They may still find something to learn from his work, they may even realize that though it is the business of architecture to deal with the present, yet architecture is a very old art, far too firmly rooted to be turned upside down by the crude experiments of those who have never taken the trouble to learn its lesson.

LORENZO BERNINI

GIOVANNI LORENZO BERNINI
From the frontispiece in the Life of Bernini by Filippo Baldinucci,
Florence, 1683

LORENZO BERNINI

In my last study I endeavoured to place Palladio as an architect, I tried to show what he stood for, and what he may still mean for us to-day. After the days of the Giants and their heroic ventures, there came the Stylist to tidy up and put everything in order; what to the earlier men had been vital means of expression were now to be formulated and even standardized. Architecture was to be put into a strait waistcoat in order to adjust it to the taste of the Virtuoso, for Palladio had made it his business to hit the taste and temper of his time and had succeeded in doing so. His work, in so far as it set up a definite standard, might have been invaluable for everybody except those rare men of genius who are a law to themselves, for it provided a definite standard to refer to, and some sort of measuring-rod by which to test vagaries of design. It was well to have this put on record, yet it was a state of things that could not last. The Italians were much too restless and versatile to acquiesce in a strait waistcoat. They soon turned their back on the Formalist and the Precisian, and indulged to their heart's content in an orgy of unlicensed architecture and sculpture. Palladio died in 1580. Within thirty years of his death the disintegration of the fabric that he had raised with such labour was complete. The attempt to prescribe the practice of art in exact detail is bound to end in failure. However much he may restrain himself, the artist is essentially a free man. Bernini and Borromini follow close on the heels of Palladio, and Borromini's extravagance was perhaps the inevitable reaction to the dogmatism of Palladio.

I am now going to discuss the life and work of a man who went to the very opposite extreme in the arts and did more than anyone to break up a great tradition. Bernini was the more dangerous, because, unlike Borromini who was an avowed and deliberate revolutionary, he posed as one in the royal line of succession, and he had an amazing capacity for success, for making the most of his opportunities with a single eye to the main chance—one will look in vain in his career for any hint of the idealism of Michael Angelo or the greater men of the Renaissance. Signor Fraschetti, who has written an admirable Life of Bernini to which I am greatly indebted, calls Bernini "the Michael Angelo of the seventeenth century". He was nothing of the sort, but he was a remarkable artist and a very interesting man. Giovanni Lorenzo Bernini was born at Naples on December 7, 1598. He was the son of Pietro de Lorenzo Bernini of Florence, an honest and competent mason-sculptor, who worked for Vignola at the great house of Caprarola, and at the age of twenty-two had moved to Naples and married a Neapolitan, Angelica Galanti. After some twenty years in Naples, Pietro settled in Rome, where he carried out a good deal of work, notably an Assumption in the Sacristy of S. Maria Maggiore, and some excellent portrait busts. Lorenzo Bernini was thus brought up from childhood in the atmosphere of a sculptor's studio, but the really important thing in his antecedents is the fact that he was born in Naples and that his mother was a Neapolitan. It is true that he was only about six years old when the family moved to Rome, but the true key to the restless extravagance, the irresistible histrionic impulse of all Bernini's art, is to be found not in the technical skill which he had learnt from his father, but in the Neapolitan temperament that he inherited from his mother. The impressions of the first few years of childhood spent in Naples, that Circe of the South, that has bewitched the souls of all her children, were indelible.

From a very early age young Bernini had worked in his father's studio, and there is no doubt that he was an unusually precocious boy. There is a story that the reigning Pope, Paul V, hearing of this infant prodigy, asked him to draw a head. Within half an hour the child, with an astuteness beyond his years, produced a drawing of S. Paul. The Pope was delighted by this subtle flattery, and it was to Paul V that Bernini owed the introduction to his great career. One of the earliest of his admirable portraits was a marble bust of this Pope, now in the Borghese Gallery. It is not an attractive head; the Pope was a big, fat man, with a heavy jowl, a sensual mouth, and a sly, rather sinister look. However, he was of inestimable value to Bernini, for he gave him an introduction to Cardinal Maffeo Barberini, who succeeded Paul as Urban VIII, and so began that Papal patronage and protection which, except for a short interval, made Bernini's career the most successful of that of any artist known to history. It was a career that began at an age when most artists are only entering on their apprenticeship, and, in spite of intrigues and the unwearied and not wholly unjustified attacks of his enemies, it lasted till his death at the age of eighty-two.

The remarkable thing about Bernini is the astonishing rapidity with which he leapt into fame, and he must have possessed some unusual quality, some rare personality, which set him apart from his fellows from the very first. His precocity was amazing. His San Lorenzo was executed when he was little more than a boy, and it was a work of obvious promise for good and for bad, the modelling is unusually skilful, the technique is excellent, but the conception is quite unconvincing, for the Saint is lying comfortably on his gridiron in spite of the flames crackling underneath; the gridiron, coals and all, is set on a thick carpet, and the flames are as unreal and insincere as the figure itself. His next achievements were a David and three groups of statuary illustrating classical subjects, Apollo and Daphne, Aeneas and Anchises, Pluto and Proserpine, commissions for Cardinal Scipio Borghese, all completed before Bernini was thirty. Of their technical ability there can be no question. They are full of vigour, the modelling is so life-like and so accomplished, that it is impossible to imagine flesh more completely realized, and yet I do not know which of his groups I dislike the most. The Aeneas carrying Anchises was the earliest and perhaps the best, in spite of the fatuous expression of Anchises, who looks a silly sort of person, not much older than his son. Then came the David, a scowling young ruffian, just about to take advantage of poor old Goliath by slinging a stone at his head before the giant was ready, a violent unpleasant figure utterly remote from the heroic grimness of Michael Angelo's David. The rape of Proserpine was completed about the year 1622. Pluto, a crowned, ugly and coarse-looking person with a ferocious squint, carries an extremely plump Proserpine in his arms. She has one hand pushed against the side of Pluto's head, but otherwise is putting up no sort of fight at all. There is a group of the same object in those quaint Mirabel Gardens at Salzburg which seems to me just as good and just as bad. The Apollo and Daphne, perhaps the most famous of all Bernini's sculpture, is characteristic of the man, and his attitude to his art. The Cardinal, Scipio Borghese, had in his collection a beautiful Greek fragment of Daphne changing into a laurel in order to escape the pursuit of Apollo. The figure, a slight girlish figure, stands upright, the arms are broken off at the elbow, but the right arm seems to have been pointing downwards and outwards; the left arm is bent as if thrust forward, the lower part of the body and the legs are already screened by the laurel branches climbing upward. The whole conception of this figure, which is illustrated in Fraschetti's book, is quiet and reticent, and pathetic in its suggestion of slim and graceful girlhood. Now Bernini had this beautiful figure to inspire him, but he produced instead this violent vulgar group, in which Daphne, a plump and rather pretty young damsel, is being swallowed up by the trunk of a tree below while, above, the hands of her stretched-out arms are most uncomfortably turning into laurel leaves. The Greek artist was content to omit Apollo altogether, but Bernini has presented him rushing up from behind, all sleek and smooth, just beaten on the post in his amorous pursuit. Now I do not underrate the amazing ability of this very popular group. Again it is impossible to imagine anything more like human flesh, or anything more accomplished so far as technical skill goes. Where in my judgment it fails is in the whole conception of the legend. Bernini has missed the poetry of the story, and he drives home his commonplace version by some rather revolting cartouches on the sides of the pedestal. Signor Fraschetti greatly admires this group, and finds in it and in the other three groups a sense of beauty and of the joy of life such as inspired the great days of classical art. That it is full of rather vulgar vigour is undeniable, but Bernini's work seems to me at the very opposite extreme to the art of the great Greek sculptors. He seems to have been wholly unconscious of the quietness, the reserve of strength that gave to that art its undying beauty, so that it defies time and is as fresh to us now as it was to the Athenians over two thousand years ago.

Bernini was a Neapolitan, the child of his time, and that a rather bad time. Michael Angelo had gone right outside and far beyond the normal thought of the art of his time, but Bernini, with all his claims to originality, was in fact the creature of the Papal court of the seventeenth century, perhaps the most grotesque travesty of Christianity that there has ever been. The Popes amused themselves by building palaces, altering and adding to S. Peter's and the churches in Rome, and they hoped to distract the attention of the populace from the fact that they were often nearly starving by setting up obelisks and constructing those fountains which are still the glory of Rome. Seventeenth-century Rome is intensely fascinating to this day, but at the time it must have been utterly conventional and incredibly corrupt, and it was of this state of things that Bernini was the exact interpreter.

In 1623 Maffeo Barberini, his early patron, succeeded to the papal throne as Urban VIII. He at once promoted Bernini to various appointments. He made him superintendent of the foundry of the Castle of S. Angelo, gave him other appointments and commissioned him to design the high altar of the church of S. Agostino, one of the best of his works of this kind, for the kneeling angels are rather charming figures, not yet the vacuous creatures of Bernini's later manner.

We now come to his first monumental work. Though only some twenty-five years old, Bernini was now recognized as the leading artist of his time in Rome. In 1624 the Pope entrusted to him the immensely responsible and difficult problem of the Baldacchino to stand under the dome of S. Peter's. The work was begun at once and took ten years to complete, and it is one of the most audacious works ever conceived, having regard to the immense scale of S. Peter's and the character of its architecture. Bernini, I think perhaps wrongly, went right away from both, and designed this fantastic canopy on quite different lines, but whether one likes it or not, the technical skill of its execution is beyond all question. An enormous amount of bronze was required for the work and also for the new cannons for the Castle of S. Angelo, so the Pope, without any remonstrance from his Architect, proceeded to strip all the bronze work off the Pantheon and had it melted down for his cannons and his Baldacchino. In order to justify himself, he had a Latin inscription set up in the Pantheon stating that these ornaments were "decora inutilia, et ipsi prope famae ignota". Indeed, one of his flatterers assured the public that it was only by divine providence that they had escaped the voracity of the Emperor Constantine, presumably in order to be melted down by the Pope. The public, however, were under no illusion in the matter, for it was said in Rome, "Quod non fecerunt Barbari, fecere Barberini". The monument was unveiled before an immense assembly in S. Peter's on June 29, 1633. The work had cost 200,000 scudi. Bernini's fees had been agreed at 34,000 scudi, a comfortable fee of some $17\frac{1}{2}$ per cent on the cost of the work, but the Pope was so delighted that he gave Bernini a bonus of 10,000 scudi, a Canonry for one brother and a benefice for another. He had already been appointed architect of S. Peter's in 1629 on the death of Carlo Maderno, and he was now let loose on the fabric with little knowledge of architecture except of its ornamental details. He proceeded to form niches in the four great piers under the dome, to be filled by large figures of saints by Il Fiammingo, Bernini himself, and two less-known sculptors, Mochi and Bolgi. The figures were fine and large, particularly the S. Andrea by Il Fiammingo and the Longinus by Bernini, but in 1636 cracks appeared in the dome and one of the adjoining walls, and the blame was laid on Bernini. All kinds of reports flew about. It was said that the church was doomed and the Vatican ruined. Bernini tried to get away with it by saying that he had made the niches by order, and did his best to ignore the attacks, but it was no good, and in the Carnival of 1638 the students carried round a model of the dome tied up with bandages. Bernini rather weakly implored them to stop, which they declined to do, and only desisted when they were ordered to do so by Cardinal Barberini. A little later when Bernini by way of scoring off Francesco Mochi, the sculptor of S. Veronica, asked him where the wind came from that blew the saint's robes, Mochi replied that the wind came from the cracks which Bernini had made in the fabric. In fact our Admirable Crichton, who claimed to be supreme in all the arts, seems to have failed seriously when it came to the hard facts of construction, and this was remembered against him and duly repeated by his enemies later on. It is only fair to say that Baldinucci, who brought out a Life of Bernini dedicated to Christina of Sweden in 1682, was at considerable pains to show that whatever Bernini may have done to the niches, the area of the four piers was so vast that this could not have affected the dome.

Bernini's position was now so strong that he could laugh at his enemies. He sailed triumphantly through the scandal of Costanza Buonarelli. This lady was the wife of his pupil and assistant Matteo, a sculptor from Lucca, and appears to have been fascinated by Bernini, who at this time, aged about thirty-five, must have been a handsome, dashing young artist. The scandal was so notorious that the Pope had to interfere. He sent the lady away, and only told Bernini to be a good boy and not do it again. Bernini had in fact behaved very badly, though he made some amends by that wonderful bust of Costanza now in the Museum at Florence, the girl with the wavy hair and wild passionate eyes. I think he must really have cared for Costanza, for he kept the bust hidden away till his marriage in 1639, when he gave it away to avoid further scandal.

Borromini, once his pupil, and now his bitter rival, might rail at Bernini and do his best to pull him down, but Bernini had the Pope's ear and was not the man to lose it. His fame was European to an extent perhaps never equalled before or since. In 1635 when Richelieu came to Rome to receive his Cardinal's hat, he had his bust modelled by Bernini, and was so pleased with it that he sent him a jewel of thirty-three diamonds, and tried to induce him to come to France and enter the service of Louis XIII, but Bernini managed to evade him and in the year following executed a bust for Charles I of England from three portraits by Vandyck. The King had written to him in most complimentary terms: "the fame of your sublime genius and of your illustrious works has passed the boundaries of Italy and indeed of Europe, and has carried your glorious name to our land of England". The Queen Henrietta sent him a diamond worth 6000 scudi, and an English nobleman is said to have travelled to Rome to have his portrait modelled by Bernini at a cost of 2000 pistoles. He was now so prosperous that at the age of forty he thought he might as well settle down, and in 1639 married Caterina Tezio, twenty years younger than himself and said to be the most beautiful girl in Rome. Caterina was the daughter of a notary in the service of the great Barberini family, and, having produced eleven children, died in 1673. Milizia, who was evidently suspicious of Bernini's youth, remarks that "from the moment of his entering the married state he conducted himself with the steadiness and propriety becoming his new character". Poor Costanza and her tragedy were forgotten, and Bernini now settled down to his rôle of an opulent and transcendently successful artist, one of the lions of Roman society and the arbiter of its taste and entertainments.

In spite of the cracks in S. Peter's, Bernini successfully defied the attacks of his enemies and rivals, and in 1637 he was given the design of the Campanili to complete Maderno's west front of S. Peter's. Drawings and models were prepared of Campanili in three stages, the two lower stages open colonnades with clusters of columns at the angles, surmounted by statues of bishops in full episcopal dress; above these was to be an open arched lantern with ogee-shaped brackets supporting a ball and a cross. It was a fantastic design, out of keeping with the massive façade of S. Peter's, but Bernini was allowed to get away with it, and was able to complete the lower stages. Then the old story of cracks and settlement was repeated, and in 1643 the work was stopped. Most unfortunately for Bernini his patron Pope Urban VIII died in 1644, and his successor, Innocent X, a Pamphili, hated the house of Barberini with a truly Papal hatred. He dropped Bernini, and appointed his rival Francesco Borromini architect for the completion of the Palace of the Propaganda, and the restoration of the churches of S. John Lateran and S. Agnese. The Pope referred the question of the completion of the Campanili to a body known as the "Congregazione della Fabrica di San Pietro", which included Borromini, Rainaldi and Martino Longhi, with Bernini as architect of the fabric. Bernini was ordered to examine and report on the foundations, and fresh designs were invited. Finally after a long discussion the Congregation recommended the destruction of Bernini's Campanili. They were taken down in 1646, and the columns used again in the Sacristy of S. Peter's and the church of the Piazza del Popolo. Bernini was threatened with costs, and it was alleged that he only escaped payment by bribing Olimpia Pamphili with a gift of 1000 pistoles and the diamond given him by the Queen of England in 1636.

Bernini was now for the first time in his life in serious disgrace, and for a time he was out of favour, so he occupied himself with a symbolical group of Truth discovered by Time, but only got as far as the figure of Truth, a fat and rather blowzy female holding in her right hand a symbol of the sun. This he left to his descendants as a memorial to the truth which would ultimately justify Bernini and all his works, an excellent allegory, but of no use as a means of livelihood, and desperate measures were necessary to re-establish his fallen fortunes. The Pope had decided to restore an existing fountain in the Piazza Agonale (Piazza Navona), and had invited designs from Borromini and others, omitting Bernini. The latter was determined to get in somehow, so he made a sketch design, and again with the help of his protectress, Donna Olimpia Pamphili, managed to have it shown to the Pope. The latter was so delighted that he gave the work to Bernini, and the famous fountain of the four rivers was the result. It was completed in 1652 after five years' work. Bernini made the design, perhaps the boldest thing of its kind ever designed and executed, for on the top of the group of the four river gods in various attitudes on the rock, he had to place a great obelisk. Bernini modelled and carved the rock himself, but he left the four figures to his extremely able assistants, the Ganges to Porissimi, the Danube to Antonio Raggi, the La Plata to Baratta, and the Nile to Fannelli. On the top of this heroic group was poised an Egyptian obelisk. The work was very unpopular. During its construction it had to be protected by guards, and as the stones were being brought to the site, the people cried, "We don't want obelisks and fountains—give us bread", for the cost was paid by a tax on the people, and then at the end there was the usual rumour that the obelisk was toppling over. Bernini dealt with this with considerable courage, for he summoned his workmen and tied up the base of the obelisk with string to the adjacent houses, to show his contempt for the outcry. This time he succeeded and the people laughed.

I think this fountain and the colonnade of S. Peter's the finest things that Bernini did in Rome. There is an heroic scale in the fountain of the four rivers that nobody but a man of big ideas could have conceived, and it is maintained throughout. Moreover, all the lower part is genuine sculptor's work, for it dispenses with architectural detail, and up to the base of the obelisk it is a noble monument. Above this the transition from the untrammelled freedom of the group to the rectangular form of the square block supporting the obelisk is not so happy.

It is to be noted in this fountain in particular how much Bernini worked through other men. At the Papal court he was supreme in all artistic matters, and he availed himself of his great position to work freely by ghosts. The four figures of the fountain in the Piazza Navona, the S. Andrea by Il Fiammingo in one of the four niches under the dome of S. Peter's, are only some among many instances, and much of the work which the casual visitor attributes to Bernini was in fact done by the very able sculptors who carried out his designs. Some of these designs were little more than hasty scribbles not particularly well drawn, for though Bernini drew a great deal and very freely, he was not a fine draughtsman, and he had far too much work to do. Yet I think Bernini really enjoyed himself in the fountains of Rome. Here he could let himself go with the exuberant vitality of the Neapolitan, and they represent the finer quality of the man, far more than his sentimental saints, his S. Theresa with the simpering angel ready to transfix her with a dart. His sensibility is not in the least convincing, it is too much in evidence and protests too much, but let him loose in a world of his own invention and Bernini was inimitable. He was not quite so happy in the two other fountains in the Piazza Navona. Il Moro is a repulsive creature, and the four tritons are dotted about in a rather meaningless way, but that sturdy little elephant in the Piazza della Minerva is delightful in its fanciful invention and its completeness as a monument. In 1665 an Egyptian obelisk had been dug up in the garden of a Dominican convent close by, and the Pope decided to set it up opposite the church. The question was how was the obelisk to be supported. Bernini made several sketches, none of them at all satisfactory, but one day he came across an illustration of an elephant carrying an obelisk in the *Hypnerotomachia Polyphili*, that strange and delightful book of the earlier Renaissance. Here was the very thing that Bernini wanted. He made a terra-cotta model, still preserved, with the obelisk resting on a sort of saddle on the elephant's back, an admirably compact design except for the careless modelling of the elephant's ears. The actual monument was executed from this model by a pupil, Ercole Ferrata, but the whole conception was that of Bernini at his best.

Innocent X died in 1655 and was succeeded by Fabio Chigi, Alexander VII, a far more genial patron than his austere predecessor, and in this year all Rome was greatly excited by the coming of Christina, late Queen of Sweden, the daughter of Gustavus Adolphus the "Lion of the North". This remarkable lady had abdicated the throne of Sweden in 1654 at the age of thirty-one, partly through boredom, partly from a restless craving for sensational action. She was clever, incredibly selfish, and callous beyond belief. Her major-domo, Monaldeschi, was murdered in 1657 by her deliberate orders, almost in her presence, and though Sweden was very poor she had spent on foreign musicians about her court, 90,000 crowns a year. She left Stockholm with all the property she could collect, and as soon as she was out of Sweden, announced her conversion to the Church of Rome. The Papal court made great preparations to receive this notable convert, and Bernini added the very ill-designed upper part of the Porta del Popolo in honour of her entry into Rome. Christina was received into the Church of Rome by Alexander VII in 1655, and when she rode about Rome two Cardinals went with her as guards of honour; but she was speedily disillusioned. She wrote to a friend that she found nothing to do but eat, drink, sleep and see the play. As for Rome it was a prey to gross ignorance and absurd superstition, there were plenty of statues, palaces, obelisks and fountains, but no men. Where, she asked, was there a Cato, a Cicero or a Caesar? The only person for whom she showed the least enthusiasm was Bernini. She visited him in his studio and treated him as a personal friend, but she could do little for him, for she was reckless and extravagant, ran through all her money, and ended her days in poverty and obscurity. When she died in 1689 they gave her a magnificent funeral in S. Peter's. Twenty thousand masses were said for the good of her soul, and so ended a quite gratuitous tragedy.

In 1656 Bernini was entrusted with the design of the colonnade of S. Peter's, by far his finest architectural work, and one which alone justifies his claim to be the very considerable architect which he believed himself to be. He took a great deal of trouble with the design. His first idea was to surround the court with a two-storey colonnade, rather in the manner of Palladio's Sala della Ragione at Vicenza, and to repeat to the north of S. Peter's, the block of buildings of the Vatican already existing on the south side. He finally settled down to the austere and stately design of a one-storey colonnade of the Doric order with an Ionic entablature and a triple way inside the columns. Owing to the projection of the Vatican buildings on the south side and the width of the west front of S. Peter's, instead of making the corridors approach from the Piazza to S. Peter's with straight sides parallel to the axis line of the church and the Piazza, the sides of the approach turn outwards from west to east, so that instead of increasing the apparent length of the vista, the perspective is inverted, and the apparent length reduced, but Bernini's intention, not carried out, had been to correct this by placing a third block in the centre opposite the west end, so that people entering the court would have looked across it diagonally. The Piazza was completed in 1668. The estimated cost of 186,000 scudi was far too low an estimate for this enormous work. The actual cost is given as 850,000 scudi. The length from the entrance at the west end to the front of the church is 366 yards, and the greatest width between the colonnades 260 yards. The figures above the columns are rather tiresome, but the Piazza of S. Peter's is perhaps the finest forecourt in the world in its noble scale and fine simplicity of treatment, and it shows more than anything the amazing range of this extraordinary man. The Piazza was followed by the Scala Regia of the Vatican, an imposing staircase with composite Ionic columns running up the stairs in a most uncomfortable way, and both here and in the Sala Ducale of the Vatican, Bernini let himself go without any restraint or regard for structural conditions. The running vault over the staircase in the Louvre designed and executed by Jean Goujon is far better than the Scala Regia, for if I may use an old-fashioned term, though he had boundless ability, Bernini had no taste. Perhaps the best example of his technical ability is the little elliptical church of S. Andrea al Quirinale one of his last works, built in 1678.

I now come to that famous episode in the life of Bernini, the visit to Paris. Colbert was anxious for political reasons to keep Louis XIV in Paris, and decided that the best way to do this was to interest the King in building, and more particularly in the completion of the Louvre. In 1665 work was begun at the Louvre from designs by Le Vau, but Colbert was not satisfied with Le Vau's designs, and consulted the architects of Paris, who condemned the design and as usual produced designs of their own. It was decided to send these designs to Rome, in order to obtain the opinions of Bernini, Carlo Rainaldi and Pietro da Cortona. The Italian architects also sent designs of their own, according to Colbert's secretary Charles Perrault "tous fort bizarres", but in spite of this, influential friends persuaded Colbert that there was only one man in the world for the work, the Cavaliere Giovanni Lorenzo Bernini, who had refused Mazarin's invitation to France twenty years before. Louis XIV himself wrote a letter requesting the Pope to order Bernini to come. The Pope granted him three months' leave, and when Bernini left Rome it is said that the whole population turned out to see him off, in their anxiety lest Louis XIV should keep him in France. Much against his will Bernini, who was now sixty-seven, set out on his journey to Paris for a fee of 10,000 scudi. He left Rome on April 29, and reached Paris on June 4 and his journey was almost a royal progress. He was accompanied by the Duc de Crequi, envoy extraordinary of France at Rome, and at Juvisy, some thirty miles out of Paris, that place with the beautiful bridge, he was met by M. de Chambray, none other than Roland Fréart, author of the famous *Parallels of Architecture*, who was officially told off to act as his guide. Bernini seems to have made his designs without any regard to the site or to the existing buildings which had to be preserved. He produced an enormous scheme which involved the destruction of all the buildings of the Louvre, with the exception of the gallery of Apollo and the galleries connecting with the Tuileries. His design provided a large central court with four smaller courts, two at each end. The elevation started with a plinth finished like rocks. Above came a rusticated ground floor and then two lofty storeys with Corinthian columns and pilasters the full height of the two storeys, an enormous and very clumsy entablature and a balustrade with the usual parade of figures on pedestals. The interior to the great court was better and might have been quite fine, but the exterior would not do at all.

Bernini's design was so far accepted that the foundations were actually begun, but nobody liked the design and the ingenious Charles Perrault drew up a report pointing out the numerous faults in Bernini's design, and incidentally the superior merits of the design by his brother Claude, which was ultimately carried out. The position was in

LORENZO BERNINI

fact impossible. The French architects were quite determined that whoever rebuilt the Louvre it should not be the Italian, and they treated him unfairly. On one occasion Bernini found Charles Perrault spying on the design for the river front, and burst into a furious rage, called Perrault a dirty dog not fit to black his boots, and told him that if he was to be insulted like this, for twopence halfpenny he would smash the king's bust and go back to Italy. Bernini seems to have realized that the game was up. He announced that he could not stand the cold and must return to Italy. He did so in October 1668, leaving behind him the foundations of an impossible building, an equestrian statue which the King disliked so much that he ordered its destruction, and that slashing, flamboyant bust of Louis XIV which still dominates the Palace of Versailles. According to Perrault and others the King rewarded Bernini very handsomely. I find, however, from the *Comptes des Bâtiments du Roi* that all that Bernini actually received was 30,000 francs advanced in Rome in 1665, and a further sum of 33,000 in June, 1666, an annual pension of 6000 francs paid him up to 1673 only, and one of 1200 francs to his son Paolo. I find no reference to the 50,000 crowns or the portrait set in diamonds said to have been given Bernini by Louis XIV. On his return to Rome, he was welcomed enthusiastically and the Pope gave him the work of completing the bridge of S. Angelo, but he was becoming old and feeble, and Rainaldi was preferred before him for the addition to S. Maria Maggiore. His last effort was the design for the monument of Alexander VII in S. Peter's, but as a composition it is all over the place. It has none of the vigour, the swagger, if I may use the term, of the great monument to Urban VIII which Bernini had put up in S. Peter's twenty years before. In that monument, instead of kneeling humbly in prayer as in the monument to Alexander VII, the Pope is shown seated on high, robed in full pontificals with hand uplifted, glaring as it seems at a terrified and bewildered people. With all its false sentiment it is rather a splendid composition, and there is a sad falling off in the later monument. Bernini's hand had lost its cunning. He died in 1680 at the age of eighty-two and was buried in the church of S. Maria Maggiore.

So ended one of the most brilliantly successful careers of any artist who has ever existed. He had had bitter rivals, Borromini, Algardi, Sacchi and Salvator Rosa, but except for a short interval he had always had the Popes at his back. In his youth he was very handsome, of ready address and of an indomitable vitality, a typical Neapolitan. He was an artist of amazing versatility. Not content with sculpture, his real art, he plunged boldly into architecture, painted several really bad pictures, wrote plays and apparently ran a theatre. He amused himself with caricatures of people he disliked, not particularly good and more malicious than humorous. He was so successful with his theatre that his rivals complained to the Pope that, owing to Bernini's monopoly, they were reduced to showing marionettes. It is always very difficult to place men of genius; in the case of Bernini it is almost impossible. Was he really a man of genius, or was he just a very clever artist with a large admixture of charlatanism? It is certain that he dealt freely in poses. It is said that he used to stand in front of his work, wrapt apparently in silent ecstasy, and would afterwards inform the bystanders that he was in love. His life shows that he was dominated by that passion for the limelight which is the besetting sin of artists of ability but uncertain character. It was this that was at the back of the persistent histrionics of his art. It impelled him to strike attitudes and gesticulate, and sacrifice everything to "la maraviglia", the motive that inspired nearly all the Baroque, and it was only a certain shrewd sense inherited from his father which saved him from that fatal obsession for novelty, that ambition to outstrip the world, which drove his rival Borromini to madness and suicide.

Yet when all is said, there is in the work of Bernini an element of real greatness. I have noted it in some of the best known examples of his work to which I have referred in this summary sketch, but perhaps the most convincing evidence of his genius is to be found in the portrait busts of the Popes and Cardinals and other great persons who swaggered about in Rome in the seventeenth century, and excited the contempt of Christina of Sweden. He was no small man who could attain to the realism of the bust of that gross creature, Cardinal Scipio Borghese, or the magnificent manner of the busts of Francesco Duke of Este, with flowing hair and drapery sweeping away into space, and its repetition in the bust of Louis XIV at Versailles. If my criticism of this famous artist may seem to be harsh, let me suggest that perhaps it is a matter of temperament and of the wide gulf that must always separate the standpoint of a casual Englishman from that of this fiery Neapolitan who wore his heart upon his sleeve. To be quite frank, Bernini's art has most of the characteristics that appeal to me least in art. It was violently self-assertive, lacking in reticence, restless and theatrical. He had no respect for his material. Indeed it was his boast that he treated marble like wax, and used the arts as interchangeable, aiming in sculpture at effects which really belong to painting. He had no consciousness of the limitation of the arts, no sense of selection, and rather vulgar, at any rate strongly theatrical, instincts. His whole attitude to the arts was that of the swashbuckler. Yet on rare occasions he could rise to great heights. His was a remarkable personality, and to some extent he fascinates one like that Baroque art which one still finds interesting however much one may contemn its follies. Partly from a certain glamour of Romance, partly from the interest that always attaches to people who kick over the traces, Bernini has something of the attraction of the Buccaneers. He stood outside the law and prided himself on doing so. A comparison of Bernini with Michael Angelo is simply ridiculous; if I may use a common phrase he was not in the same street; but Bernini did some very big things; he was typical of his time and place, and he remains to us an artist of first-rate interest, from his failures not less than from his astonishing success.

INIGO JONES

INIGO JONES
From a limewood medallion in the Victoria and Albert Museum

INIGO JONES

I NOW come to a great English artist, who, unlike Bernini, had none of the advantages of coming far down in a long succession of men of genius and supreme attainment. When he began his amazing career, Bernini had ready to hand a technique that had been built up by many generations. Brunelleschi, for example, had designed the church of Santo Spirito in Florence just two hundred years before Bernini designed the Baldacchino of S. Peter's in Rome, yet the Corinthian capitals of the nave of Santo Spirito are more correct than those of the Baldacchino. All that there was to be known of Neo-classic architecture, as based on the ruins of Rome, had long been familiar. Vignola and Palladio had reduced it to a system, and Italian craftsmen were perfectly familiar with its detail, so that they could carry out whatever they were called upon to do almost as a matter of course. In other words, the Italian architects of the seventeenth century had inherited a complete technical equipment which they could use as they liked, and in some cases used quite recklessly.

Inigo Jones, the subject of my discourse, was in an entirely different position. Such tradition as existed in England at the beginning of the seventeenth century was a debased and Germanized version of Neoclassic. He had to find out everything for himself, and he had to introduce a complete reform of architecture into a country conservative by instinct and ill-prepared to receive the teaching of an alien culture. To understand what Inigo Jones did for English architecture, it is necessary to go back a hundred years and consider what was the state of the art in England in the sixteenth century, and we shall then be able to realize that, for good or bad, Inigo Jones gave an entirely fresh direction to English architecture, and set it on a path that it was to follow for the next two hundred years. Wren's brilliant achievements and the accidents of history have drawn a veil over the work done by Inigo Jones, but in actual fact Wren's career was an interlude and an interruption in a tradition which began with Inigo Jones in the reign of James I and ended with Sir William Chambers and the break-up of the classical tradition towards the end of the eighteenth century.

The accidents of history play an unfortunate part in the reputations of artists. There is always the tendency to sweep all works of merit and of unknown authorship into the net of the one most eminent or best advertised man of the period. Also, there are the actual circumstances of history, such as the Civil War in England, in which records are destroyed and men are forgotten. Few great artists have suffered more in this regard than Inigo Jones, who still remains more or less a "magni nominis umbra".

In actual fact we know little of Inigo Jones, and of his predecessors practically nothing at all. Down to the beginning of the sixteenth century buildings were carried out on traditional lines, often with very charming results. One recognizes in them the hand of some unknown artist; moreover, they are essentially English. They reveal that temperament which is one of the best traditions of the Englishman, reticent and undemonstrative, yet endowed with a deeper sentiment than is to be found in the brilliant rhetoric of Italy. Houses, for example, such as Haddon Hall or Compton Wynyates nestling in its fold in the

Cotswolds, are typical in their restfulness and their absolute sense of home. But buildings such as these were the swan-song of a dying tradition. It was doomed when Italian artists and craftsmen invaded France and England, and the whole orientation of Western art was changed. Early in the sixteenth century, needy but capable Italian craftsmen found in the Courts of France and England employment which they could no longer obtain in Italy, and the "new fashion", as it was called, backed by King and courtiers, came in with a rush. Unfortunately these men were not architects but just ornamentalists, and when Henry VIII thought he was well in the movement, he was under the same illusion as Francois I and the wealthy financiers of France who built their châteaux on the Loire. They were given, not Italian architecture, but Italian ornament plastered on to buildings designed and built on a wholly different tradition. Nonesuch, that sumptuous palace that Henry VIII put up near Cheam, was a characteristic example. It consisted of two large courts, surrounded by two-storey buildings; the ground floor was built of stone, the upper storey was of half-timber with posts and quarters covered with lead and gilt, and "richly adorned and set forth and garnished with a variety of pictures and other antick forms of excellent art" to quote the description of the Commissioners who dismantled Nonesuch in Cromwell's time. The fabric was built by English workmen in the manner of their country, but the ornamentation was carried out by foreigners, and the whole thing was just the caprice of an extravagant amateur which led nowhere. Then came the break of Henry VIII with Rome, the Italians gradually left the country, and their place was taken by the industrious Fleming and German, with their dreadful pattern books by Wendel Dieterlin, de Vries and others, and their foolish ornament of strap-work, bulging balusters, foolish little orders, and the whole paraphernalia of Elizabethan and Jacobean ornament which disfigure what might otherwise have been innocent and attractive buildings—Audley End, Hatfield, Wollaton and Bolsover are characteristic examples. Orders were used for no purpose but that of surface ornament, as for example Bodley's Tower in the schools at Oxford, where the mason was evidently determined to show that he knew all about the orders, Doric, Ionic and Corinthian, and could pile them up one above the other as well as anybody else, but this was not architecture, and never would be. These men knew nothing of the Italian editions of Vitruvius by Fra Giocondo and Daniele Barbaro, or of such excellent handbooks of the orders as those of Vignola, Palladio or Serlio. They relied on Hans Bloome's orders, Vries's perspective, Wendel Dieterlin's architecture, and so far no trained architect had detached himself from the crowd to exercise some control over the uninstructed taste of the builder and the amateur. England had no Alberti or Peruzzi or Palladio, not even a De l'Orme, or Jean Bullant. Robert Smithson, the designer of Wollaton, and his son Huntingdon of Bolsover were the best it could show till the coming of Inigo Jones. The famous houses built in the reign of Elizabeth are often picturesque, and always interesting on account of their historical associations. Also, when all is said, they still reflect in certain aspects the bold swagger of the Elizabethan age, but they are not great architecture, and they show no grasp of the essential principles of that art, fine planning and composition, considered proportion, and the translation of practical purpose into ordered design. So far as I am aware, there is no real evidence for the existence of any English architect, as we should now understand the term, in the sixteenth century. The architect had not yet emerged from the general body of craftsmen as an independent designer who devotes his life to the designing of buildings and the superintendence of their construction. John of Padua is almost mythical and did not build Longleat. Sir Reginald Bray probably arranged for the building of the Henry VII chapel, but he certainly did not design it. John Thorpe surveyed existing buildings and left a valuable collection of the results of his surveys, and he may have acted as a superintendent of buildings, but the evidence does not warrant the assumption that he was an architect, and if he was, he only followed the existing habit of the time of Elizabeth. The Smithsons were not much better. There is little trace in the works of these men of any knowledge of Italian architecture beyond the rudimentary and garbled versions presented in the Flemish and German handbooks.

I must quote myself. "No necessity was felt for a trained designer, and the method of building by rough contracts with the trades, who supplied the designs and executed the work, continued in common use till the end of the sixteenth century and in some places a good deal later. So long as son succeeded father with an uninterrupted tradition of craftsmanship, the system answered its purpose in a modest way, but when, as happened in the sixteenth century, all kinds of new motives were in the air, first Italian, then Flemish and German, there was need of some person of wider knowledge and more discerning taste to control the aberrations of the workmen." As the old tradition derived from medieval times faded away, there was nothing to take its place. The meaning of the new architecture was misunderstood in far-away England, and people who had heard of it, and hoped to follow it in their houses, had no conception of the real meaning of the new departure. They supposed it to consist of the substitution of one set of ornament for another, and did not grasp the fact that for good or for bad it meant a definite change in the standpoint of architecture. Only a man of genius could clear the air, someone with clear vision, enthusiasm and a resolute will, who could rescue English architecture from the quagmire into which it seemed to be content to settle. Inigo Jones was that man, he came out of space as it were, he had to find his way, and do so at first without any powerful patrons to back him, yet before he died in 1652 he had revolutionized English architecture.

Inigo Jones was born in Smithfield in 1573. His father was a clothworker in St. Bartholomew's, Smithfield, who died in 1596, apparently in rather straitened circumstances, and this is all we know of the first twenty-five years of the life of his son. There is no record left of where he was educated, of what it was that called his attention to architecture, where he learnt it, even of how he learnt to draw and become the consummate draughtsman that he was in later years. In an anonymous memoir, written a hundred years later, it is said that he was "early distinguished by his inclination to drawing and design, and was particularly taken notice of for his skill in the practice of landscape painting". In the Chiswick collection there is a landscape attributed to Inigo Jones rather in the manner of Gaspar Poussin, and some vigorous landscapes in pen and ink. It seems that as a boy he was apprenticed to a joiner in St. Paul's Churchyard. Ben Jonson, with whom he was closely associated in the Masques at Court, and who later on regarded him as a hated rival, refers to this in the *Tale of a Tub*:

> And he named me " In and In Medlay which serves A joiner's Craft . . . . but I am truly Architectonicus Professor, rather That is as one would say, an Architect."

The *Tale of a Tub* is one of the dullest of Ben Jonson's plays, written after 1631, when he was an old and bitterly disappointed man. Elsewhere he jeers at Inigo Jones as a Somersetshire man, and there seems to have been some sort of family connection with Budleigh in Somerset. But there is no record of his early training. Somehow or other he managed to get to Italy before the end of the sixteenth century. He says himself in his *Stonehenge Restored*, "Being naturally inclined in my younger days to study the arts of design I passed into foreign parts to converse with the great masters thereof in Italy".

Palladio's four Books on architecture had been published some thirty years before. At the end of the sixteenth century this was the accepted text-book in Italy, and it was fortunate that Inigo Jones visited Italy at a time when the strictest tradition of Neo-classic still held the field in Italy, and the hooligans of the Baroque had not yet begun to pull it to pieces.

Again we know little or nothing of this first visit to Italy, and there is a good deal of confusion about Inigo Jones' visits to that country. He was certainly there twice, once at the end of the sixteenth or beginning of the seventeenth century, and again in 1614. My impression is that Inigo Jones made a long stay in Italy during his first visit. Webb, his pupil, writing in 1668, says definitely that he had "resided many years" in Venice, and I think it must have been during these years that he learnt his architecture, based on the work and treatises of Palladio, whose reputation was supreme in Venice at the end of the sixteenth century. From Venice he could easily reach Vicenza and study the works of his master, both there and in the neighbourhood of Venice. In Venice he must have attracted attention by his vigorous personality and his obvious ability as a draughtsman, and Christian IV, King of Denmark, heard of him and summoned him to Copenhagen, where, according to the tradition, he is supposed to have designed three important buildings, the Castle of Frederiksborg, the Rosenborg Palace and the Exchange, but it is nearly certain that he had nothing to do with any of these buildings. They are in the manner of the country and show little trace of Italian influence, and it is impossible to imagine that Inigo Jones, a young man full of enthusiasm for the austere and scholarly art of Palladio, could have designed that Tower with dragons' tails entwined. As a fact, with the exception of the Frederiksborg Castle, these buildings were begun after Inigo Jones had left Denmark, and the architect of Frederiksborg was a certain G. F. Stahlmann. All that is known for certain is that he was for a time in the service of the Danish Court before 1604, probably as a draughtsman employed to put Christian's ideas into shape, for that amiable Sovereign fancied himself as a designer, and there is no art so convenient for the noble amateur as architecture, in which the ghost can make all the designs, and the noble patron such as Lord Burlington signs the drawings and claims the buildings as his own invention.

Still, it was certainly to Christian of Denmark that Inigo Jones owed the opening of his career, for that King introduced him to his sister Anne of Denmark, wife of James I of England. The Queen appointed Inigo Jones her architect and he thus obtained a footing in the English Court. He returned to England not later than 1604, for on Twelfth Night 1605, the *Masque of Blackness*, composed by Ben Jonson, was performed at Whitehall "of which the bodily part was of Master Inigo Jones' design and art", and when in 1605, James I was the guest of the University of Oxford, the University called in Inigo Jones to design the "mise en scène", and obtained the assistance of two of his Majesty's carpenters and a foreman for the construction of the stage. Anthony Wood says, "They also hired one Mr Jones a great Traveller, who undertook to further them much, and furnish them with rare devices, but performed very little of that which was expected. He had for his pains as I heard it constantly reported 50£."

In 1605 Inigo Jones was thirty-two years old, and evidently enjoyed a considerable reputation, not, however, as an architect, but as a man who had travelled widely and was supposed to have learnt all sorts of new fashions in Italy and elsewhere. He had seen Palladio's theatre at Vicenza, and must have heard of the temporary theatre that Palladio had designed for the performance of *Hyrcanus, King of Jerusalem* by the Company of the Calza at Venice. He had probably heard of Peruzzi's inventions for the stage, and the technique of the theatre in Italy was far in advance of anything in any other country. In England the resources of the stage were quite rudimentary. There was no moveable scenery, its place was taken by "nuncupations", labels and inscriptions, such as "This is a tree", to inform the audience what was the intention of the playwright. Inigo Jones, who had seen strange things in Italy, introduced a new and wonderful world to the English Court. Instead of a stage in the middle of the audience, he set back the stage behind a frontispiece as he had seen it in Palladio's theatre at Vicenza, and for moveable scenery he had painted slips or "shutters" as they were called, with ingenious machinery for changing them as desired. He introduced all sorts of devices for lighting with and without colour, sumptuous and fantastic dresses designed by himself, and for actors he had the Queen herself and the most eminent Lords and Ladies of the Court, for all these changes were confined to the Court, and it was the Masques played at Court in the reign of James I and the earlier years of Charles I that gave Inigo Jones his opportunity. Here is Ben Jonson's description of "The House of Fame" in the *Masque of Queens*, given at Whitehall on February 2,

1609, by the "Queen of Great Britain and her Ladies". I give it in full because it is typical of the sumptuous magnificence of this phase of the Renaissance, its glory of display, its reckless extravagance, and the strange world of romance in which from time to time it delighted to lose itself. Ben Jonson writes: "There rests only that we give the description of the House of Fame, the structure and ornament of which was entirely Master Jones' invention and design. First for the lower columns he chose the statues of the most excellent poets as Homer, Virgil, Lucan, as being the substantial supporters of Fame. In the upper, Achilles, Aeneas, Caesar, and those great heroes whom these poets had celebrated, all which stood as in massey gold. Between the pillars underneath were figured land battles, sea-fights, triumphs, loves, sacrifices, and all magnificent subjects of honour, in brass and heightened with silver, in which he profest to follow that noble description made by Chaucer of the place. Above were sited the masquers, over whose heads he devised two eminent figures of Honour and Virtue for the arch. The friezes, both below and above, were filled with several coloured lights like emeralds, rubies, sapphires, carbuncles, the reflex of which with the light placed in the concave [footlights] upon the masquers' habits was full of glory. These habits had in them the excellency of all device and riches, and were worthily varied by his invention to the nations whereof they were queens. Nor are these alone his due, but divers other accessories to the strangeness and beauty of the spectacle, as the hell, the going about of the chariots, and binding the witches, the turning machine with the presentation of Fame—all of which I willingly acknowledge for him, since it is a virtue planted in good natures, that what respect they wish to obtain fruitfully from others they will give ingenuously themselves,"—a handsome tribute to Inigo Jones, but, alas for these amiable sentiments, in another thirty years we shall find Ben Jonson doing all he could to make Inigo Jones ridiculous. Both of them were proud, arbitrary and unyielding men. Ben Jonson became jealous of the amazing success of his colleague. He felt that the beauty of the architect's scenery interfered with close attention to the poet's verse, and the rift between the two widened with every Masque.

After 1625 the name of Inigo Jones appears as "inventor" before that of Ben Jonson, and after 1630 Ben Jonson wrote a bitter attack on Inigo Jones. He charged him with incompetence and imposture, ridiculing his affectation of scholarship, "his twice conceived thrice paid for imagery". In view of possible honours he suggested, "We'll have thee stiled the Marquis of Townditch", and ended his invective with the bitter line, "Thy forehead is too narrow for my hand".

The limits of this short study do not allow me to go further into this fascinating subject of the Masques played at Court and elsewhere in the reigns of James and Charles I. The *Masque of Blackness* was the first; the last, by Davenant, was entitled *Salmacida Spolia* and was played at Whitehall in 1639, its object being to express the King's desire "to reduce tempestuous and turbulent natures into a sweet calm of civil concord". The Parliament replied in 1640 by an ordinance of both Houses for "the suppression of public stage plays throughout the Kingdom during these calamitous times".

It seems that on the suggestion of her brother, Christian of Denmark, Inigo Jones had been appointed architect to the Queen soon after his return from Denmark and he was already in the royal service, as in 1609 he was employed as a King's Messenger to France. In 1610 he was appointed surveyor to Henry, Prince of Wales, for whom he did certain work at Richmond in connection with Solomon de Caux, the designer of waterpieces and fountains, but he does not seem to have been employed as an architect till 1616, the date of the earliest signed architectural drawing by Inigo Jones. Prince Henry died in 1612, and Inigo Jones paid his memorable second visit to Italy very soon afterwards. It appears from the entries in his annotated copy of Palladio now in the library of Worcester College, Oxford, that he was at Vicenza in January 1614, and it seems that for about a year from the middle of 1613 onwards, he was living in Italy, at Rome, Vicenza, Tivoli and elsewhere. He paid a flying visit to London early in 1614, possibly to receive instructions from his patrons, the Earls of Arundel and Pembroke and Lord Danvers, for whom he was collecting works of art, but his main object was the study of classical architecture. He spent long days amid the ruins of Rome, checking and correcting his Palladio, noting his own observations and making bitter comments on the vandalism of Papal Rome. He refers to the authorities up to date—Serlio, Vignola, Fontana and Labacco, and also to the prodigious treatise of Philibert De l'Orme. He mentions a talk with Scamozzi on August 1, 1614, but had a very poor opinion of Scamozzi, who was a pupil of Palladio. He accused him of ignorance and malice against his old master, and noted that "in this as in most other things else, Scamozzi errs". Vincenzo Scamozzi, who had a great reputation in Venice, had already completed his vast book of architecture, and published it at Venice in 1615. Inigo Jones suspected him of trading on the deserved reputation of Palladio. Bernini and Borromini were boys in 1614, and Inigo Jones does not refer to them. It seems, however, that he knew some of the famous architects of the time at Rome, and Ben Jonson's gibes at his scholarship were not entirely justified. He had of course not the erudition of that remarkable poet and playwright, but I doubt if any architect of that time made as close and sympathetic a study of classical architecture as Inigo Jones.

On his return to England he was appointed Surveyor-General of the works at a salary of £80 a year, with 8s. a day allowance, and 2s. 8d. for travelling and riding expenses, and this was really the beginning of his career as an architect at the age of forty-two. In 1617 he prepared the designs and model for a new Star Chamber, and began the Queen's House at Greenwich, still the most perfect and beautiful example of his work. In 1618, he prepared a plan for the layout of Lincoln's Inn Fields. In 1619 came the great opportunity, the commission to prepare designs for the new Palace of Whitehall. The Banqueting-Hall alone remains, and it was from one of its windows that on a bleak January morning thirty years later, Charles I was to go out to his death on the scaffold.

There is a great deal of confusion in the accounts of this memorable design, because Campbell published one set of designs in his *Vitruvius Britannicus*, 1717-25, and William Kent, the tame architect of Lord Burlington, published another set in 1727 from drawings in his Lordship's possession. The explanation is that two sets of designs were made; the designs published by Campbell were Inigo Jones' draft made in 1619 for James I, and the only part of this that was carried out was the Banqueting-House, completed in 1622. The original plan was an oblong rectangular block in three compartments, a central court 392 by 198 feet, with subordinate courts on each side, divided into three, the central court on the right-hand side being circular in plan on the inner side. The building was to have been in two storeys with orders above orders, the Ionic below and the Corinthian above. James I was a thrifty Scotsman. His son Charles I was not at all satisfied with this relatively modest palace, and at some date after 1630 instructed Inigo Jones to reconsider the whole scheme. That architect carried out his instructions by simply doubling the size of the palace. The total area in the design made for James I was 630 by 460 feet. In the design made for Charles I this was increased to 1280 by 950 feet, more than double. The famous Persian court, the circular court in the centre of the right-hand compartment, was to be 280 feet in diameter, and the height of the centre block was to be about 110 feet. It was an ambitious scheme, far greater than anything that had ever been thought of in England, or indeed anywhere else, for De l'Orme's palace of the Tuileries, designed and built some sixty years before, was on a much smaller scale, and though there were immense Castles here and there in England, they were the result of the accretions of centuries, not designed at one time as one vast new building.

It is evident that Inigo Jones had studied De l'Orme's plan closely, and he adopted some of his motives, but in the elevation Inigo Jones went right away from the Frenchman, and designed his palace in the true Palladian manner, but on a scale and with a feeling for the grand manner beyond anything that Palladio had ever attempted. The Banqueting-House, mere fragment though it is of a gigantic design, and in spite of mutilations, is not inferior to the finest work of Palladio and the Italian architects of that time, and it should be recollected that this belongs to the first design, not to the tremendous scheme prepared for Charles I, but never carried out. To his own countrymen it must have been a startling revelation of what Neo-classical architecture meant if rightly handled. Its design was based on the practice of Palladio. The motive of the carved frieze below the entablature lineable with the capitals of the columns, was borrowed from the Palazzo Thiene at Vicenza, but the whole conception of this great palace was due to the genius of Inigo Jones, and it is an important landmark in the history of English architecture.

From 1619 onwards, the date of the first design for Whitehall, Inigo Jones was constantly employed by the King on Royal Commissions and superintendence of buildings. In 1626 he designed the Watergate of old York House, which still survives, half buried, at the foot of Buckingham Street, and this was carried out by his faithful friend Nicholas Stone the elder, mason and sculptor. In 1630 he was made a Justice of the Peace for Westminster, much to the indignation of Ben Jonson who addressed him thus in his "expostulation": "By all your titles, and whole style at once—of tireman, mountebank and Justice Jones—I do salute you". In the next year he designed the church of St. Paul's, Covent Garden (since rebuilt), "the finest barn in Europe", as he described it, and he was now called in to rebuild the Cathedral of St. Paul's, which was in a lamentable state and partly ruinous. Laud had succeeded in raising over £100,000 for the purpose; the work was begun at the west end, for which Inigo Jones designed an entirely new façade, and he had progressed eastward as far as the south transept when the work was stopped by the Civil War, and Parliament annexed what was left of the money collected by Laud. In order to clear the site for his new design, Inigo Jones had, in a very arbitrary way, pulled down the church of St. Gregory in 1637 in spite of the protests of the parishioners. He was summoned before the House of Lords, and had to hand over his materials to the parishioners for the rebuilding of their church. The Queen's House at Greenwich was finished in 1635, and he followed this up with designs for a royal palace at Greenwich, which Wren adopted and altered when he came to design the palace for Charles II which is now Greenwich Hospital. In 1637 he made a fine design for the rebuilding of Somerset House, part of which was carried out, and probably the last of his works in London was Lindsay House in Lincoln's Inn Fields, built in 1640. The Civil War broke up his career. In 1643 he was dismissed from all his appointments, and soon afterwards, having buried his money and possessions in Lambeth Marshes with the help of Nicholas Stone, he fled to Basing House in Hampshire, where he spent the next two years with Hollar, Faithorne the engraver, and Robinson the actor. The house was taken by Cromwell in 1646, and Clarendon says that Cromwell put most of the garrison to the sword. Inigo Jones got off with the payment of a heavy fine, and seems to have been left alone by the Parliament men, for in the next year he made some additions to Kirby in Northants, and Ford Abbey in Wiltshire and probably designed Coleshill in Berkshire, and possibly Raynham in Norfolk, though the latter is very doubtful. In 1647-48 he designed the buildings on the south side of Wilton which contains that splendid double cube room 60 by 30 feet with the portraits by Vandyck, probably the most perfect room of its kind in England. This seems to have been his last work. He died on June 21, 1652, and was buried by the side of his father, in the church of St. Bennet, Paul's Wharf.

The authentic work of Inigo Jones is in fact very scanty, and there is little or no evidence for some of the buildings attributed to his design. His name disappeared in the years that followed the Civil War, and as is shown by the treatment of his pupil and son-in-law, John Webb, he was forgotten by Charles II and his Court. Important people after the Restoration tried to forget not only Cromwell and the Puritans, but all those unhappy years in which the reign of Charles I had ended. Moreover Italy was now a dead letter and the Court looked to France for its enlightenment in fashion and the arts. So for some fifty years Inigo Jones and all that he had done for architecture was ignored. Yet the Queen's House at Greenwich, the Banqueting-Hall and the south wing at Wilton are sufficient to justify the claim of John Webb that "it was *vox Europae* that named Inigo Jones, Vitruvius Britannicus, being much more than at home, famous in remote parts". He was technically by far the most accomplished architect this country had produced. The staircase of Ashburnham House shows his technical ability. Whatever his failings as an antiquary, he had by incessant study learnt all that there was to be learnt at that time of the scholarship of his art. His work has been little recognized on the Continent, and nowadays it is almost forgotten in England, yet the austere distinction of his style, "his masculine and unaffected manner", to use his own words, place him high not only among the architects of this country, but among the famous architects of the world. He was a consummate draughtsman, a master of perspective, with an invention and resourcefulness that anticipated the work a hundred years later of those amazing theatrical designers and perspectivists, the brothers Bibiena. The drawings and designs for the scenery, figures and costumes of

Masques in the Duke of Devonshire's collection at Chatsworth will show how far ahead he was of our modern theatrical designers.

It is difficult to form a personal impression of architects such as Palladio and Inigo Jones. As Leoni complained in his preface to his translation of Palladio, "we are told all about their buildings, but nothing about themselves". Inigo Jones was forgotten during the Civil War, and after the Restoration his fame was overshadowed by the extraordinary career of Christopher Wren. The notes that he left in his writings are technical, and little can be learned as to his personality, either from these notes, or from his gratuitous guesses as to the origin of Stonehenge. If we are to believe Ben Jonson, Inigo Jones was a harsh, arrogant man, who claimed a knowledge which he did not possess, and was given to an affectation of scholarship peculiarly irritating to a man of the genuine erudition of Ben Jonson. That Inigo Jones completely took the wind out of Ben Jonson's sails in the matter of the Masques at Court is evident, and this explains the poet's rancorous hatred. It is also clear that Inigo Jones was arbitrary and high-handed in his methods. His brilliant success at Court may to some extent have turned his head and would certainly have rendered him unpopular with rivals for the royal favour, for whatever his virtues, Inigo Jones was not the meekest of men, and, finding himself in the saddle, had no intention of being thrown out of it. One can sympathize with the bitterness of Ben Jonson when he realized that people then as now were more interested in the spectacle provided by the master of the stage, than they were in the verses of the author of the Masques. I gather also that Inigo Jones was not free from a common weakness of artists, and of men of genius even, who have risen out of space to social eminence, that of inordinate vanity. Yet there remains the work that he did. He introduced order into chaos, rescued English architecture from the tangle in which a hundred years of ignorant experiment had left it, and brought it back from a merely provincial manner to the main lines of that Neo-classic architecture which had begun far back in distant Italy. He did the same thing with the stage, for the "mise en scène" of the modern theatre in England began with the changes introduced from Italy by Inigo Jones at the beginning of the seventeenth century. He remains to this day one of the most important figures in the history of English architecture. In the Victoria and Albert Museum there is a medallion portrait of Inigo Jones carved in lime-wood. It shows a man of about forty years of age with the face in profile, a fine romantic head with deep-set eyes under overhanging eyebrows, rather high cheek-bones, a beard and moustache, and natural hair magnificently treated. I take this to be Italian work, probably executed during the second visit of Inigo Jones to Italy, and it suggests the man as I conceive him to have been, not the mountebank presented by Ben Jonson, not the smug professional man or the unscrupulous thruster, but a passionate artist of high imagination, ever moving onwards in pursuit of his ideals. It is a tragic face, because it is that of a man who was hopelessly out of touch with the spirit that was moving over the face of England; of a man too impetuous to stand back from his work and take account of what was going on around him. Yet fifty years later he came into his own in England, and he remains a great and outstanding figure in English architecture, for those who care for fastidious scholarship and the finer qualities of the art.

The present fashion turns its back on these

things. It is not interested in personality, and offers us a standardized architecture which might as well be a composition in packing-cases, painting and sculpture which attempt to formulate things outside the range of those arts, music which is little more than noise and discord, and prose and poetry which are now deliberately unintelligible. A generation has arisen that knows not Joseph, that in its impatience has no use for the past, and expects those of us who have had experience of better things to accept their crude experiments and theories as the last word in the arts. They forget that the world is very old, that what has been will be, and I suggest to this generation that they may still learn something from the life and work of artists such as Inigo Jones, an Englishman of genius, who laid the foundation of all that was best in our architecture for the next two hundred years. They will learn also that what really lasts in the affection of mankind is not the result of mass production, but the effort of the individual, the personal contribution of the artist. After all, what interests us in art and literature is not what everyone thinks, but what one exceptional person thinks, how he reacts to the constantly recurring problems of life, and his individual version of his own reactions. The standardized art which our social, economic and artistic reformers hold up as the ideal to be aimed at is a contradiction in terms. If art is not personal and individual it is nothing.

FRANÇOIS MANSART

FRANÇOIS MANSART
From a portrait by Namur, engraved by Edelinck

FRANÇOIS MANSART

In the history of French architecture, François Mansart stands by himself, and holds a position somewhat analogous to that of Inigo Jones. They were contemporaries. Both men were technically far ahead of their time, but here the resemblance stops, for Inigo Jones, who revolutionized English architecture, did so, coming out of space, as it were, and deliberately Italianized English architecture, whereas François Mansart had behind him a definite and unbroken succession of trained architects, going back for at least a hundred years. His people were connected with the building trades; he was trained as an architect by an architect in the royal service, and unlike Inigo Jones, he never went to Italy. His genius was essentially French, both in its invention and expression, as racy of the soil in its own way as Amiens Cathedral is in quite another manner. I think of all civilized peoples, the French were the most tenacious of their national idiom in the arts. After the initial change they were less influenced by

Italy than any other country, and we shall find that in this regard his great successor, Ange Jacques Gabriel followed faithfully in François Mansart's footsteps. I am convinced myself that every people has its national idiom in the arts, and that as soon as it loses touch with that idiom and plays with cosmopolitanism, it is on the road to Babel.

The worst of attempting to give an account of architects is that nobody seems to have thought it worth while to tell us anything about them. The sad truth is that architects have never caught the attention of the public to anything like the same extent as painters and sculptors. It is true that many architects are just professional men, not artists, but even with the rare artists among them, there is an abstract quality in architecture which makes less appeal to the lay mind than works of painting and sculpture, and this is the more regrettable because architecture is or should be the Mistress art that, in its highest expression, orders and directs the other arts, allotting to each their share in an organic whole. But architecture is the Cinderella of the arts, and those who have tried to find for her the golden slipper have seldom been Princes out of Fairyland. François Mansart is a case in point. Charles Perrault, who included him in his *Hommes illustres*, a short account of distinguished Frenchmen of his time, and who might have talked with Mansart himself, only knew that he was born in Paris in 1598, the year, by the way, in which Bernini was born in Naples, that his father was an architect who died young (he was in fact a carpenter), that he was apprenticed to his brother-in-law, and that he possessed an exquisite taste, a solid and profound intelligence, and an ambition to go one better than anyone else. Blondel, the famous professor of architecture in the eighteenth century, who had an immense admiration for François Mansart, said that the Mansart family came from Rome, had been settled in France for eight hundred years, and had for generations served the kings of France as architects, painters and sculptors, a well-meant but rather foolish attempt to glorify his hero on quite irrelevant and wholly hypothetical grounds. Most unfortunately for François Mansart, his fame was lost in the blaze of glory that encompassed the younger Mansart, the architect of Versailles. The older and the younger Mansart should be completely separated. François Mansart the elder was an austere and most distinguished architect, Jules Hardouin Mansart the younger an extremely able and successful adventurer.

François Mansart was the son of Absalom Mansart, a carpenter in the royal service, and the only training he received was from Germain Gautier, a relation by marriage, who was killed in an accident in the building of the Parliament House at Rennes in 1636. The only other known Mansarts were Jehan Mansart and Pierre his son, who were employed on the Louvre and Tuileries as sculptors at the beginning of the seventeenth century, probably uncle and cousin to François. Mansart had no influential backing to start with, and he owed his rise to his own genius, but he was fortunate in his country and his time. Throughout the seventeenth century, from the days of Henri IV till the latter years of the reign of Louis XIV, everybody who could afford it was building a house in France, and there was an uninterrupted tradition of the new manner of design in France dating back to the beginning of the sixteenth century. The introduction of Italian artists into France in the reign of François I had been a much more serious affair than the attempts made in England by Henry VIII.

With the mere ornamentalists had come competent architects such as Serlio, and almost first-rate artists such as il Rosso and Primaticcio at Fontainebleau. Quite early in the sixteenth century in France the mason contractors had given place to trained architects, who had taken over the design and control of buildings, De l'Orme, Bullant, the du Cerceau family, De Brosse and others, who had laid down on firm and permanent lines the foundations of Neo-classic architecture in France. There was a "détente" at the end of the sixteenth century owing to civil war, but matters settled down again with the establishment of Henri IV on the throne of France, and though Salomon de Brosse tried a clumsy reversion to Italian architecture to please Marie de Medicis, a true vernacular classic had already established itself in France early in the seventeenth century. This was carried on without a break by able architects such as Pierre Le Muet, the architect of Bussy-Rabutin Tanlay in Burgundy and some excellent houses in Paris, and by that very competent architect Jacques Lemercier, the architect of the great Château of Richelieu, and of that delightful little town of Richelieu near Chinon, the only example of a town built at one time and from the designs of one architect. I must quote myself: "The advance in architectural sense shown in Lemercier's work as compared with that of Bullant and De l'Orme, is scarcely less than that of those valiant pioneers on the work of the builder designers of François I. We at length approach the period of complete development after something like 150 years of experiment. The technicalities of Neo-classic, the orders and the details of architectural ornament no longer presented any difficulties to the architects of Louis XIII. The architects of the Grand Gallery of the Louvre, of the Luxembourg, of Richelieu, the men who designed the Place Royale and the Porte et Place de France, had little to learn in the conduct of great enterprises in building. Yet with one exception they were not quite past-masters of their art. The subtleties of proportion, the vital quality of scale, the virtue of reticence in ornament still eluded them, and we look in vain for unity of effect and the one essential phrase. It was reserved for François Mansart to set the seal of genius on French Neo-classic architecture."

The whole history of Mansart's early years is obscure; there are no records to explain how he could have made a reputation, such that when twenty-two or not much older, he was entrusted with the design of the Hôtel de Toulouse (now the Banque de France) and the flamboyant west front of the church of the Feuillants in Paris, built in 1624 and destroyed in 1804. We only know this front from engravings of the time, and if Mansart really designed it, he very soon dropped this ambitious manner, and settled down to the definite quest of the finer qualities of architecture. He was not much more than twenty-five when he designed the great house of Balleroy in Normandy, built from his designs between 1626 and 1636. Balleroy is one of the best country houses of the reign of Louis XIII in France and a characteristic example of the manner of Henri IV, which dispensed with external ornament, and all the paraphernalia of the orders applied to façades, on which so much time and money had been wasted a hundred years before, for this great house relies for its effect on its excellent proportion, symmetry and composition. In the centre is the main pavilion, three storeys and attics flanked by two-storey wings, then comes a break, and two one-storey pavilions standing apart and in advance of the main work, the whole building set up on a stone terrace with an open-work balustrade. Mansart may have proceeded from this to design the Châteaux of Cany Barville, Miromesnil and Dauboeuf in Seine Inférieure and the fine house of Berni, now destroyed and known to us only through Perelle's engraving, but these attributions are all a little doubtful and one must take as typical of François Mansart's manner his authentic work at Blois, at Maisons and the Val de Grace. In or about 1630 he was appointed architect to Gaston de France, Duc d'Orléans, a wretched creature who was always intriguing against his brother, Louis XIII. Gaston had been pardoned and reconciled to the King by Richelieu in 1630, and given the governorships of Amboise and Orléans with considerable payments in cash, but in consequence of his persistent disloyalty he had again to flee from France, and it was not till 1635 that he was again pardoned and able to return to France from Brussels. He signalized his return by instructing François Mansart to prepare plans for the demolition of the Château of Blois, one of the finest buildings of the reign of François I, and to rebuild it to a totally different design. All the north-west side opposite the entrance was pulled down and, barbarous as one may think the proceeding, Mansart built in its place what is perhaps the best example of Neoclassic domestic architecture to be found in France. The composition is very simple. As at Balleroy, in the centre there is a pavilion rather higher than the adjacent buildings. A colonnade, of coupled Doric columns on a curved plan, connects the main building with the wings, and above the colonnade the building continues for two more storeys. The great slate roof sweeps round with a continuous line, unbroken by dormers. At either end the building is left unfinished, and it is evident that it was intended to continue it all round the courtyard, but the work was never completed, for Gaston took part in all the plots against Richelieu, played a miserable part in the Fronde, and died in 1660, disliked by everyone. The most notable thing in Mansart's work at Blois is the magnificent stone staircase. This occupies an oblong compartment 36 by 30 feet. The stairs stop at the first floor, the walls above are carried up to a bold cove cornice richly decorated with sculpture, all in stone, and leading up to a large oblong opening recessed and returned on the long sides, with a balustrade round the opening. Above the cove is a landing forming a gallery round all four sides, and above the landing the wall is continued on an oval plan with recesses for the windows, and terminates in an oval dome with a cupola. The whole of this is carried out in stone, with an admirable sense of scale, and it is a masterpiece of masonry such as only the French masons of the seventeenth and early eighteenth centuries could build, dependent for its stability on ingenious combinations of straight and curved arches and the counteraction of their resultant thrusts. Inigo Jones had designed a small flying stone staircase on a circular plan in the Queen's House at Greenwich, and he seems to have been playing on this motive when he designed the beautiful staircase of Ashburnham House, but what Mansart had done in stone Inigo Jones had to carry out on a much smaller scale in wood and plaster. Mansart's work at Blois has been condemned as cold and uninteresting as compared with the Salamanders and Fleur de lis and other ingenious details of the Château of François I, but this criticism is inspired by the inveterate error of mistaking ornament for architecture. The austere reticence of Mansart's building at Blois will always appeal to those who care for the great and permanent qualities of architecture.

Mansart's next important work was one of the most famous houses of France, Maisons on the left bank of the Seine, some thirteen miles north-west of Paris. René de Longeuil, President de Mortier of the Parliament of Paris, a man of great wealth and unscrupulous ability, determined to build himself the finest country house in France. In 1642 he took Mansart down to Maisons to discuss the site and the building, and Mansart undertook the work on condition that if he did not like what he had done and thought he could improve on it, he should be allowed "carte blanche" to alter as he thought fit. De Longeuil actually agreed to this, and the rebuilding of one of the wings in accordance with this agreement cost him 100,000 livres, but he was justified of his choice, for Maisons both then and ever since has been considered to be the best thing of its kind in France. He is said to have spent on the house and grounds, all of which Mansart designed, 12 million livres, and the best sculptors and painters of the time were employed on its decoration. As shown in Perelle's views, in front of the house there was a fine forecourt, surrounded by a moat and double balustrade, continued all round the house. The general plan consisted of an oblong block with a pavilion in the centre on the garden side, carried up above the rest of the building, and smaller pavilions at the ends. On the entrance front, in the principal block there is a lofty centre pavilion as before, and at either end, pavilions advanced beyond the main block containing oval chambers, one of which was a chapel, the first example of those oval or circular rooms which afterwards became very popular in French domestic architecture. The length of the façade of the main block is about 240 feet. The whole building is absolutely symmetrical, and in spite of all that has been done by subsequent owners to mutilate the house, Maisons is still in its beautiful proportions, in the subtlety of its planes, in its perfect sense of scale and values, a consummate masterpiece. Its later history is characteristic of many of the great houses built round Paris in the seventeenth and eighteenth centuries. In 1777 the last of the house of de Longeuil sold the property for less than a quarter of what it had cost his ancestor to build. The Comte d'Artois tried to induce Louis XVI to buy it, by suggesting that if he pulled down the château, he could extend the forest of St. Germain right down to the Seine. In 1804 Lannes, Duc de Montebello, one of the best of Napoleon's marshals, bought the property for 400,000 francs, and amused himself by planting poplars to represent the position of the troops in one of his victories. Lannes was killed at Essling, and finally in 1818, Mme de Montebello, his widow, sold the property to Jacques Lafitte, a wealthy banker, who pulled down Mansart's stables, replaced the panelling in the house with wallpapers of 1825, destroyed what was left of the gardens, and in 1834 broke up the park into building plots. The banker ruined himself by his speculations, and after his death his executors sold the property in 1849 to a M. Thomas, who with the help of an "architecte paysagiste", designed what he supposed to be a "jardin anglais" and put the finishing touch to the barbarities of Lafitte. It is now the property of the State, but when I last saw it some twenty-five years ago it was in a deplorable condition. The forecourt was a waste of unkept grass, not a vestige of the garden remained, the house was occupied by a caretaker and his dogs. What was once the avenue of approach is now dotted about with detestable little villas, Moorish houses, Swiss chalets, and the like, and to realize what Maisons once was, one must refer to Perelle's engravings. The French, with all their elaborate Ministry of Beaux Arts, seem to be sometimes criminally careless of their beautiful buildings of the past. They either restore them so completely that the historical interest of the building is lost, as at Pierrefonds and Carcassonne, or they forget all about them, and I know no sadder instance of this than their neglect of Maisons. Berni, a fine house on lines rather resembling Maisons, now destroyed, is attributed to Mansart, and though there is as usual a sad lack of trustworthy historical evidence there is no doubt that Mansart was now, at the age of fifty, extensively employed in designing town houses in Paris, and country houses in its neighbourhood, for wealthy financiers and other important persons. In that rare and beautiful little volume of engravings, "desseignez, mesurez et gravez par Jean Marot, architecte Parisien," and known as "Le petit Marot", there are plans, sections and elevations of a large house built from the designs of Mansart for the Commandeur du Gers or du Jars; Marot seems uncertain as to the spelling of the name. Du Jars was a somewhat futile person who narrowly escaped execution by Richelieu for his share in one of the intrigues of Mme de Chevreuse, and on another occasion was bonneted with his own soup-tureen. The house was destroyed in 1851. Its plan was remarkable for the completeness of its arrangements, with several service stairs in addition to the grand staircase, and internal areas for light and air, a great advance on the house-planning of the time, for Mansart was a beautiful planner. It is to be noted that when he altered the Hôtel d'Argouge, now Hôtel Carnavalet, he carefully preserved Goujon's admirable sculpture on the façade.

Unlike Bernini and, in a less degree, Inigo Jones, François Mansart possessed the rare virtue of appreciation of the past. Blondel says of him, "If Mansart's great capacity were not known throughout all Europe, the care that he took to preserve the masterpieces of Jean Goujon would have been enough to render eternal the memory of this illustrious man". "How many architects", he continues, "far inferior to Mansart have buried admirable work in oblivion, for fear that it might destroy their own productions, or from some ridiculous vanity of supposing that anything not carried out in their time and under their own orders was not worth preserving." I commend this last sentence to the attention of our Modernismists for whom the past has no meaning. Most great artists throughout history have had a reasonable respect for the past; they have taken the trouble to study it closely and learn its lesson, and until and unless our modernists follow their example, and learn that traditionalism is a wholly different thing from revivalism, their efforts are likely to recoil on their own heads as merely futile experiments.

Mansart's superiority over his colleagues, including even that able and successful architect, Lemercier, is as evident in his design for churches as it is in his domestic architecture. His early work at the church of the Feuillants has gone, but there still exists in the Rue St. Antoine the Church of Ste. Marie, one of the most remarkable churches in Paris and by far the most original. Mansart had to deal with a very difficult site, almost square, bounded by other buildings on the east, west and south sides and the Rue St. Antoine on the north. Instead of following the immemorial plan of nave, aisles, transepts and choir, Mansart solved the problem by designing a church with a circular nave 42 feet 6 inches in diameter, surrounded by chapels. The entrance from the Rue St. Antoine is on the axis line north and south, and is faced by a chapel at the opposite end reached by seven steps. On the transverse axis east and west are two chapels reached by seven steps, and from these chapels a narrow passage leads to small elliptical chapels on the diagonals, with balustrades of bronze on black marble overlooking the central nave. Set around the nave and between the openings to the chapels, single Corinthian pilasters 2 feet 9 inches wide support an entablature, from which the dome rises directly to a lantern and cupola without any intervening drum. The floor is paved with black and white marble quarries radiating from the centre. Ste. Marie was converted into a Protestant church and is now shabby and neglected, but as Mansart left it, this church must have been a beautiful example in Neo-classic architecture of a church on a very unusual plan. Its fine simplicity of treatment, the lighting, screened as it is behind the openings to the chapels, yet ample for its purpose, and the perfectly adjusted scale and proportion throughout, give a peculiar dignity to what is in fact a rather small building.

Except for the chapel of the Valois at St. Denis now destroyed, and De l'Orme's chapel at Anet, no attempt had been made in France to design a church or chapel on a circular plan. At Rome the church of St. John of the Florentines designed by Michael Angelo, though very different in treatment, has a somewhat similar plan, which may have suggested the plan of Ste. Marie to Mansart, but he is not known to have ever been in Italy and no illustration of that church existed till De Rubeis published his series of plates of the churches of Rome in 1683, yet the plans are so much alike that I think Mansart must have heard of the church in Rome.

Mansart had now reached that critical part of his career not unknown to architects, when having been recognized by his contemporaries as the first architect of his time in France, his reputation began to fade away, partly owing to the intrigues of a younger generation anxious to take his place, but also it must be admitted to Mansart's own intransigence. There came the tragedies, first of the Val de Grace and then of the Louvre. Anne of Austria, who founded the monastery of the Val de Grace in Paris, had registered a vow to build a magnificent church on the birth of the Dauphin, afterwards Louis XIV. Mansart prepared the designs, and in 1645 Louis XIV, then a child of seven, laid the first stone. The general idea was to treat the church as a great monument, forming the centre-piece of the grand court of entrance, with lower buildings on either side, returned along two sides of the court. The church was entered from the court by a broad flight of sixteen steps, and all the part up to the first parapet appears to have been built to Mansart's design, but at this point Anne of Austria appears to have lost her nerve and her confidence in Mansart. The work was taken out of his hands and entrusted first to Lemercier, who carried it up to the top of the square below the drum of the dome, then to Le Muet, who with the help of Le Duc, an inferior architect according to Blondel, took all sorts of liberties with Mansart's design, and produced the unsatisfactory dome with its drum and lantern. All this part of the exterior is rather unattractive, but the interior justifies Blondel's praise, for it is one of the rare Neo-classic interiors, which avoided on the one hand the banalities of the Jesuit church, and on the other the frigid accomplishment of pedantic classic. Blondel went so far as to say that he knew no church of which the interior was so inspiring to the faithful, and so entirely satisfactory to "les hommes de bien," persons of condition, a remark characteristic of the time of Louis XV. Mansart's dismissal by Anne of Austria seems to have been the turning-point of his career. His enemies attacked him for his reckless extravagance, accused him of robbing his clients, and a pamphlet entitled *Mansarade*, which appeared in 1651, went so far as to say that he had been threatened with the rope at the Palais Mazarin, for having nearly destroyed the building. That there was no foundation for these malicious attacks is proved by the fact that when Colbert was considering the completion of the Louvre in 1662, the first architect that he consulted was François Mansart, and Colbert, much the shrewdest man of his time in France, would not have had anything to do with Mansart had there been any truth in these libels. What really happened was that Mansart, a great artist and a hopeless idealist, made himself impossible. The story is very well told in Perrault's *Hommes Illustres*: "This excellent man", he says, "could never satisfy himself, and when he was working, better ideas would occur to him, and he would remake his design again and again, when something more beautiful presented itself to his imagination. Colbert sent for Mansart and asked him to bring with him his designs for the completion of the Louvre. Mansart opened his portfolio, and showed the minister several designs 'tous très beaux et très magnifiques' but none of them finished, one in pencil, another in ink and another in red chalk. Colbert expressed himself as greatly pleased with the beauty and abundance of these ideas, but added that Mansart must decide which of these was the best, complete the design and submit it to the King, after which all would be well. But Mansart replied that he could not tie his hands and that he must reserve to himself the right to alter his design as he went on, if he saw that he could improve it, to which Colbert replied (I think with his tongue in his cheek, for he was a thrifty person) that if the building was one for himself, he would let Mansart pull it down and build it again eight or ten times, if he desired to do so, but as it was a question of a building for the King, and the building was the Louvre, it was impossible to agree to Mansart's conditions." So the whole thing fell through, Colbert tried Le Vau, then dropped him and sent for Bernini, and after the French architects had succeeded in getting rid of the Italian, Colbert's secretary, Charles Perrault, succeeded in securing the work for his brother, Claude, an exceedingly able man who, by the way, was a Doctor by training, and died in 1688 of blood-poisoning, caught in dissecting a camel for the Academy of Science.

Mansart died in 1666 with a reputation overshadowed by the rising generation, and most of all by Jules Hardouin, the most successful and unscrupulous thruster among any architects known to history, whose real name was Hardouin and who seems to have been a nephew by marriage of François Mansart. Saint-Simon says that Jules Hardouin tacked on his great uncle's name of Mansart to his more humble name of Hardouin "pour se faire de réclame", in which it must be admitted he was entirely successful, for to most people the name Mansart only suggests Jules Hardouin Mansart, the architect of Versailles. François Mansart's career had been unusual. From an obscure position, without influential friends to send him to Italy, he had built up for himself a great reputation and was recognized in France as the first architect of his time. Inigo Jones had done this in England, and Bernini in Italy, and indeed in Europe, but Bernini certainly, and I think Inigo Jones to a certain extent, had all the qualities that lead to success, great ability and resourcefulness, a quick eye for a chance and no hesitation in seizing it. So far as one can judge from their portraits, both Bernini and Inigo Jones were sanguine, high-handed men. Mansart was very different. I take him to have been one of those rare men who are born with an unerring instinct for fine quality, a man who, in his search for it, was indifferent to immediate success, and to all those other thorns that so often spring up and choke the artist's ideal. His independence, his absolute claim for a free hand, impracticable as it obviously was, show that his whole being was concentrated on the perfection of his art, but it also meant his downfall. Refined and sensitive to the highest degree, François Mansart was lost among the adventurers who crowded the Court of Louis XIV after the middle of the seventeenth century. Blondel, the famous eighteenth-century professor, has a fine panegyric of Mansart: "François Mansart", he says, "may be considered the most skilful architect that France has ever produced. All the productions of that illustrious man are remarkable for their purity and severity. Few indeed are struck with this perfection .. they even regard with indifference this beautiful simplicity and repose ... and are unmoved by that correctness which fixes our reason, satisfies our intelligence and inspires us with a reasonable and considered admiration for all that is beautiful. Nowadays—people prefer the difficult, the singular, the extraordinary" (he was thinking of Oppenord with his cutlets and colifichets), "but what an abuse of architecture this is. Of all the arts architecture is the least susceptible of variety ... artists should search deep in the sources of what is truly beautiful, and should recollect that those ancient buildings which have acquired immortality, have only done so, because they have always been recognized as beautiful by really competent judges." This is a little too close to "quod semper, quod ubique, quod ab omnibus", and Blondel did not allow for the inevitable changes of architecture involved by changes in life, but his critical judgment was right. Mansart stands apart from his contemporaries and successors in the singular completeness of his art, his sense of scale, his instinct for proportion, and his fine simplicity of statement. He stands in French architecture where Inigo Jones did in English, and Baldassare

Peruzzi in Italian. Each of these men was, first and last, an artist, and their qualities were those which, when abler men of affairs have been forgotten, will make future generations turn to them again, as artists who have preserved their ideals untarnished to the end.

ANGE JACQUES GABRIEL

ANGE JACQUES GABRIEL
From a bust by J. B. Lemoyne in the Louvre

ANGE JACQUES GABRIEL

An attractive chapter in the history of French architecture closes with the death of François Mansart. It began in the reign of Henri IV, most liberal and patriotic of all the later kings of France, and it ended with the coming of Colbert. The freedom and initiative which Henri of Navarre had encouraged continued under Richelieu and Mazarin. Under those ministers there was no drastic interference with the arts, and architects, as we saw in the case of François Mansart, were free and independent to a very remarkable degree. With the rise of Colbert this freedom and independence disappeared. Not only was the practice of architecture henceforward to become strictly professional, but it was made a branch of the State service, controlled by the iron hand of Colbert, and in a less degree by his successors. Mazarin was not particularly interested in the arts, and though that astute Italian had accumulated an immense personal fortune, he had left the finances of the State in hopeless confusion. The King was being robbed right and left, the system of farming out the taxes led to all sorts of abuses, and the first step that Colbert took when he succeeded Mazarin was to introduce a definite system into the finances of the State and to reconstitute the very loose organization of State officials. The case of Fouquet was one of many instances not only of maladministration but of actual malversation. Having cleared the air by the removal of that minister, Colbert began a far-reaching reorganization not only of finance, but of the staff in the royal employment. The administration of the royal buildings had been incredibly wasteful. Colbert introduced a system somewhat analogous to that of an Office of Works, which enabled him to control the royal buildings, architects, contractors and all down to the last sou. The "Architectes du Roi" were now to be something more than a name, and Colbert added to the Academy of Painting the Academies of Sculpture and Architecture, with the highly important subsidiary school of the French Academy in Rome. It was part of Colbert's policy to keep the young King in Paris, in order to distract his attention from wars and dangerous adventures, and divert it to the more harmless enterprises of building. Hence the completion of the Louvre and the extravagant palaces that followed, and hence the highly efficient staff which Colbert placed at the disposal of the King. Henceforward everything was to be regimented and subordinated to the glory of the King as the embodiment of the State. The result was a close ring of architects in the employment of the Crown such as J. H. Mansart, Robert de Cotte and the Gabriels, and it was exceedingly difficult for anyone not connected with the reigning clique to break into that ring. Some of the best of them, such as Daviler, gave it up in despair, and retired from Paris to the provinces. There can be no doubt that Colbert's reforms were of immense service to the arts of France, and gave them that technical pre-eminence in the art of the civilized world that French art has never wholly lost. For a time also, and in the first flush of enthusiasm, the new organization worked well, but it was inevitable that it should stifle the individual, and put in his place a professional and even an official class of undoubted competence and invincible monotony. With the exception of the orangery at Versailles, which I attribute to Desgodetz, any part of that enormous building might have been done by anyone of the "Architectes du Roi". In the latter part of the reign of Louis XIV, political and financial difficulties led to a slackening off in building, and in the eighteenth century, in spite of lotteries and Law's desperate remedies, these difficulties were constantly increasing, yet the tradition remained that everything was to be done for the glory of the King, no matter whether the treasury was bankrupt and the people starving. The Royal Staff of Architects maintained their position and the three Academies clung to their privileges and monopolies, till they were all swept away in the Revolution. Though it is still very attractive and of extraordinary distinction, the art of France in the eighteenth century was based on an unparalleled condition of corruption, servility and intrigue, culminating in the control of the arts by the King's mistresses, Mme de Pompadour and her successor, Mme du Barri. In one way the painters and the sculptors were better off than the architects, for the architects were not free men, and were under the heel of a formidable official, the "Surintendant des Bâtiments du Roi", a sort of first Commissioner of Works, whose office had been established by Colbert and invested with very extensive powers. Thus the conditions under which Gabriel worked were different from those under which François Mansart had worked a hundred years before, and in some ways a good deal more difficult, but Gabriel had the immense advantage of being born in the purple. He belonged through his relations to the ruling clique, for he came from one of those French families in which the practice of architecture and the business of building were hereditary.

From early times it had been the custom in France with middle-class families to adhere to their professional tradition from generation to generation, and in an informal way to build up an intimate society which almost took the place of the old guilds of mason builders. The families of the Du Cerceau, Dorbay, Hardouin, Mansart and De Cotte are familiar examples, but the most remarkable instance was the Gabriel family. A Gabriel was at work on the town hall of Rouen early in the seventeenth century, and the dynasty lasted, ever growing more powerful and wealthy, down to the death of Ange Jacques Gabriel in 1782. His grandfather, Jacques Gabriel, "Architecte et entrepreneur des Bâtiments du Roi", had married in 1663 Marie De Lisle, a niece of François Mansart, and on the occasion of her marriage the old architect had presented the bride with a gift of 3000 livres tournois. Their son, Jacques Jules Gabriel, born in 1667, was an excellent architect, who designed the Hôtel de Ville at Rennes, an admirable building, the Évêché and the bridge at Blois, the cathedral at La Rochelle and the Place Royale, or Place de la Bourse at Bordeaux, one of the finest examples of eighteenth-century municipal architecture in France, altogether a considerable man and a worthy successor to François Mansart. He was faithful to the tradition of keeping all profitable work in the family and its circle, for in 1688 when quite a young man he had bought the post of "Contrôleur général alternatif" of the royal buildings, gardens, tapestries and manufactures from Jules Hardouin Mansart, his cousin by marriage, for the sum of 80,000 francs, a gross and shameless job, for Jacques Gabriel was hardly of age at the time of the purchase. However, he justified his position, and died in 1742 full of honours, a Chevalier of the Order of S. Michael, Siegneur de Bernay, Inspector-General of the royal buildings, the ablest French architect of his time, surpassed by only one French architect in the eighteenth century, his son, Ange Jacques Gabriel.

Ange Jacques Gabriel was born in 1698, just a hundred years after the birth of Mansart in France and Bernini in Italy. He was the son of Jacques Gabriel by his second wife, whose marriage contract had been signed by no less eminent persons than J. A. Mansart the Archbishop of Rouen, a Cardinal and the Maréchal de Lorges. Ange Jacques had at any rate a magnificent start, so far as his connections were concerned, but nothing is known of his early training. He may have studied under De la Hire and Desgodetz, the latter a superb architectural draughtsman, in the school of the Academy of Architecture in Paris, but where he really learnt his business as an architect was in the various hotels in Paris and other buildings carried out from his father's designs, for there can be little doubt that apprenticeship in the office of a skilful architect, with study and observation of the actual work carried out from his designs, is a more efficient training than any that can be given in a school, because it brings the student into touch with the actual realities of building, and does not put the cart before the horse. The result in the case of Ange Jacques was excellent. His father was a fine architect, and he thus escaped the taint of vulgarity seldom absent from the work of Jules Hardouin Mansart and his followers. The strange thing is that young Gabriel never went to the French Academy in Rome. He seems to have started at once with his father and, like François Mansart, his design is purely French, with little trace of Italian influence, for the Italians at the beginning of the eighteenth century were knee-deep in the Baroque, and the influence of Oppenord and Meissonnier was only a passing fashion, which the logical sense and fine taste of the French rejected after a burst of extravagant experiment.

In 1728 Gabriel married Catherine de la Motte, daughter of the first Secretary to the Duc d'Antin, who had succeeded J. H. Mansart as "Surintendant des Bâtiments du Roi", a useful step on the road to official promotion. As a marriage gift his father handed over to him the important post of "Contrôleur des Bâtiments du Roi". In the same year he was elected an Associate of the Academy of Architecture, so here he was at the age of thirty nearly at the top of the tree, holding as

"Contrôleur des Bâtiments du Roi" a great position in the official hierarchy, and an Associate of the Academy of Architecture. Seven years later he became a full Academician, and on the death of his father in 1742 he was appointed "premier Architecte du Roi", with a lodging for life in the Orangery of the Tuileries, and the King gave him a site for a house at Versailles. He had been closely associated with his father in the work at Rennes and Bordeaux, but he was now to have his first great opportunity of work on his own, the Place Louis XV, now the Place de la Concorde. After the Peace of Aix-la-Chapelle in 1748 the Provost and "Échevins" of Paris decided to put up a monument to the King, as a mark of the "zeal, affection and gratitude of his people", many of whom at the time were without bread to eat. Bouchardon was to be entrusted with the monument, and the King was to select the site. An open competition was held and more than fifty designs were submitted on sites all over Paris. Many of the Academicians entered the competition, but all the designs were rejected on the ground that they involved the destruction of existing property. A fresh competition was held in 1751, for which all the members of the

Academy of Architecture entered with the exception of old Robert de Cotte, who was said to be too old and too rich, and seven others. De Vandieres, brother of Mme de Pompadour and afterwards Marquis de Marigny, who had succeeded his uncle as "Surintendant" in 1751, reported unfavourably on all the designs, including Gabriel's, which, according to him, destroyed the "bel accord" between the Tuileries and the Champs-Élysées, and De Vandieres produced a design of his own which would he said get over all the difficulties. Fortunately the amateur was put back in his proper place. Louis XV, who with all his vices was no fool, and knew something about architecture, presented the waste piece of ground between the Tuileries Gardens and the Champs-Élysées, and handed over the work to Gabriel. Gabriel's plan was finally approved in 1753, with "further modifications" in 1755, when a new street was included in the scheme, the Rue Royale, leading up to the site of the present church of the Madeleine. Gabriel treated the site as a forecourt to the gardens of the Tuileries. The monument of the King was to stand in the centre of a "Place" 750 by 522 feet, surrounded by balustrades. Outside the balustrade was a dry moat 54 feet wide and 14 feet deep, with the balustrade repeated on the outer side. There were to be three openings on the west side, one to the Champs-Élysées, one to the existing avenue of Cours la Reine to the south-west, and one to a similar avenue to the north-west. At the four external angles there were to be pairs of "guérites", little guard-houses admirably designed, versions of which were reproduced not very successfully in the new forecourt of Buckingham Palace. On the north side, Gabriel designed the façades of the two blocks right and left of the Rue Royale. The Garde-Meuble is on the right. Here he followed the motive of Perrault's façade of the Louvre, and again showed his independence of Italian architecture and his loyalty to French.

Gabriel's design for the Place Louis XV was a splendid scheme, and excepting Bernini's colonnade of S. Peter's, was the finest thing of its kind yet done. In its present state, the Place de la Concorde gives little idea of what the effect must have been as left by Gabriel. Perronet the Engineer had already proposed in 1787 to fill up the moats with the spoil from the foundations of the new bridge over the Seine, and in 1836

Hittorf did away with the moats, put up the obelisk and rostral columns with complete disregard of the original design, and at the same time replaced the groups with which Gabriel had crowned his "guérites" with the lumbering figures of the cities of France. Those groups by the way represented those virtues which, with unconscious irony, were claimed as the basis of the government of Louis XV.

Gabriel's deserved reputation now rests on three works, the Place Louis XV, in spite of its subsequent mutilation, the École Militaire, part only of a magnificent scheme, and the Petit Trianon. Throughout the eighteenth century France was in ever-increasing financial difficulty. The State on occasion made efforts to recover its balance by futile expedients such as official lotteries, yet in spite of this, money was wasted on all sorts of caprices of the royal mistresses, and when serious works were undertaken they were constantly held up because there was no money available to pay the contractors. Indeed on one occasion when the École Militaire was being built, Mme de Pompadour advanced the money herself in order to stave off a strike.

The École Militaire, intended for the training of the sons of officers, was suggested by Mme de Pompadour, who wanted to find something to interest the King. A very able report was drawn up for her by Paris Duverney, a well-known financier of the time. The establishment was to have been on a gigantic scale. It was to provide for five hundred students, each to have a room of his own, fifty officers each with a separate suite, stabling for fifty or sixty horses, an infirmary, chapel, lodging for guests, doctors, nurses, apothecaries, tailors, bootmakers and so on. It was to be complete and independent, the latest thing in hygiene and equipment. Gabriel duly prepared his design in accordance with Duverney's specification, but the cost was so enormous that the whole thing had to be cut down. In 1756, there were only two hundred students instead of five hundred, and a lottery was held to finance the building. Only the centre block of the main court was built, and in this the pavilions at either end of the façade were omitted. The chapel (now or till recently used as a military store) was placed in one of the wings instead of standing free. The work dawdled on and the beautiful grand staircase was not finished till 1773, twenty-two years from the date when the work was started. The École Militaire is thus only a fragment of the great scheme devised by Gabriel. Yet incomplete as it is, it is technically one of the best buildings in France. Gabriel possessed to an astonishing degree that sense of architectural values, that instinct for proportion and reticence in design, which I have already noted in the case of François Mansart almost alone among French architects, and like Mansart he was faithful to the French tradition. The great square dome, which forms the centre-piece of the façade of the École Militaire, is a reminiscence of what had been done a hundred years earlier at Cheverny. It is indeed the last word of a tradition that it had taken some two hundred years to form, a tradition which, as the Comte de Fels, the biographer of Gabriel, says, ought never to have been abandoned, and which is now lost beyond recall.

Gabriel must have had an exceedingly difficult time in carrying out his work. There was never enough money. The "Surintendant" himself reported that the royal houses were again becoming ruinous, as they had been in the time of François I, that the contractors were at their last gasp, and the workmen usually on strike. Yet the King went on ordering new buildings, alterations to his palaces, an opera-house at Versailles, hunting-boxes for himself, a Brimborion at Rambouillet, a Hermitage for Mme de Pompadour at Fontainebleau, the Petit Trianon at Versailles for Mme du Barri, and so on, and this was not the worst of it, for Gabriel had to contend with all sorts of difficulties thrown in his way by that powerful person, the "Surintendant des Bâtiments". Marigny, who had succeeded his uncle, de Tournchem, in this office, might have said "my uncle chastised you with whips but I will chastise you with scorpions", for his relations with Gabriel, "premier Architecte du Roi", were dominated by a persistent determination to get the architect under his heel. De Tournchem had tried to insist that Gabriel should submit to him every detail. Gabriel had replied that this interference was dishonouring to him as an architect, that the Architect ought not to be let and hindered in carrying out his work, and that confidence in the Architect was essential if his work was to be successful. De Tournchem had to shift his ground, and excused himself to Duverney by saying that any difficulty that had arisen at the École Militaire was due to Gabriel's vanity and ambition, but he had to give way. His successor, Marigny, was a more dangerous adversary. Through his sister Mme de Pompadour he was very powerful. He had travelled in Italy, and assumed that on this ground he knew all about the arts, a not uncommon delusion with amateurs, and that he was therefore entitled to interfere with architects and other artists who really did know what they were doing. He had failed in his efforts to supersede Gabriel at the Place Royale, and he seems to have made a point of trying to head him off at every opportunity. Moreover he was none too scrupulous in his methods. Matters came to a head in 1767. Marigny had tried to force a protégé of his, De Wailly, an architect, not only into the Academy, but into the position of full member without passing through the preliminary stages of Associate. The Academy of Architecture very properly rejected De Wailly; thereupon peremptory instructions were sent to the Academy ordering that body to place De Wailly in the class of full members. The Academy, led by Gabriel, again refused. Marigny, who had been taking the waters at Spa, was furious, and on his return to Paris had "lettres de cachet" sent to all members of the Academy of Architecture, prohibiting them from calling themselves "Architecte du Roi", and announcing that the Academy would be suppressed, and reconstituted on an entirely different basis. So far the Academy had stuck to its guns with excellent courage, but the "lettres de cachet" were formidable, and in order to avoid the threatened extinction of the Academy, Gabriel headed a deputation to the King at Compiègne, and a compromise was arrived at by which De Wailly was admitted to the first class, but it was placed on record that this was not to be regarded as a precedent. This was a somewhat lame conclusion, for the Academy was clearly within its rights, and by accepting this compromise was violating its own constitution, but the Academy before the Revolution was a Court affair and this submission to Court dictation, and the failure to stick to their principles, was but another step to their dissolution a little later on. Gabriel had led the Academy of Architecture in its protest with characteristic energy and ability, but he seems to have failed at the last fence. I suppose the pressure of his colleagues was too much for him. They probably felt that if the Academy was dissolved, they themselves would vanish into oblivion.

Marigny was not in the least reconciled by this surrender. He made a savage attack on Gabriel later on, when Gabriel was acting as arbitrator on a question of plagiarism between two draughtsmen, one of whom complained that Gabriel's man had stolen his work. Gabriel gave his award in favour of his own man, and Marigny accused him of a gross abuse of his position, but Marigny was not a man to be trusted. He himself had filled Menars, the large country house near Blois which had been left him by Mme de Pompadour, with costly furniture, tapestries and the like, which were in fact the property of the State.

Throughout the latter part of his career, Gabriel was constantly occupied with additions and alterations at Versailles. The Opera House was built from his designs. It was begun in 1748. As usual it was not completed till twenty years later, and instead of the sumptuous marbles that J. H. Mansart had had at his disposal, Gabriel had to make his columns of wood and paint them to imitate marble. He took infinite pains with his decorative scheme for the Opera House, a harmony of green and gold, with touches here and there of grey and yellow. A description of 1827 says that the columns were lighted from inside through pieces of coloured glass, to give the idea of a jewelled surface. Apart from this the scheme sounds attractive, the very opposite of the repulsive decoration that replaced it in the restorations of 1837. Versailles as left by J. H. Mansart seems to have been very uncomfortable, and Gabriel had remodelled some of the rooms, and provided further accommodation by removing the Escalier des Ambassadeurs in 1752. About this time a much more extensive scheme for the conversion of the palace, known as "Le Grand projet", was discussed, but nothing was done till twenty years later, when Mme du Barri, anxious to show that, like Mme de Pompadour, she also was an enlightened patroness of the arts, induced the King to take up the scheme. "Le Grand projet" was to destroy the Cour de Marbre and rebuild it on very much larger lines in harmony with Mansart's design. The Cour de Marbre was all that was left of the old hunting-box of Louis XIII. Mansart and others had always wanted to destroy it, but Louis XIV, much to his credit, absolutely refused to have it touched, out of regard for his father's memory. In 1772 Louis XV, who was rapidly failing, agreed to "Le Grand projet", and the work was begun, Mme du Barri actually advancing money herself, but there was not enough, and in 1773 the workmen struck. Mme du Barri was so furious that she asked that they should all be sent to prison, but the wise old architect told her that he thought "le remède un peu fort". The King died in the following year, the work was stopped and the Cour de Marbre survives to this day. The wastefulness of the reign of Louis XV is incredible. The Louvre was neglected, but a vast scheme was prepared for the completion of the palace of Compiègne in 1751. It was begun but not completed in 1775, and it almost seems that, had it been possible, Gabriel would have been prepared to rebuild to his own design the enormous palace of Fontainebleau. He did actually pull down the right wing of the "Cour du Cheval blanc", containing the famous gallery of Ulysses painted by Primaticcio, and rebuilt it in brick and stone, and he also designed the fine pavilion overlooking the lake, in the Cour des Fontaines, but again a fine historic building was saved by lack of money.

We are near the end of a great career, and almost the last work that Gabriel did was the Petit Trianon, generally admitted to be one of the masterpieces of Neo-classic architecture. This beautiful little building is usually associated with Marie Antoinette, but in point of fact it was designed by Gabriel for Mme du Barri, who resided here till the death of Louis XV. The site had been occupied by a farm for cows and poultry, with an octagon pavilion in the middle of the grounds, designed by Gabriel for Mme de Pompadour. In 1763 this was removed and replaced by the existing building from Gabriel's design. Mme de Pompadour died in 1764, and Mme du Barri came into possession, and held it for ten years, till she was cleared out by Louis XVI on his accession to the throne in 1774. The Petit Trianon became the favourite playground of Marie Antoinette, and to this it owes its survival, for Louis XVI was so scandalized by his father's relations with Mme du Barri that in 1774 he ordered the demolition of all buildings connected with that unfortunate lady. The Petit Trianon was indeed the last word of Gabriel's art, summing up all the great qualities of his design, his instinct for proportion, his sense of values and his fine selection in ornament. The Comte de Fels says that this building marks the moment when Greek art came to purify

French architecture, and that its design is at once "Hellenic" and French. He points to the report on the monuments of Greece, made by the architect Le Roy in 1758, as the starting-point of the Greek movement which came into fashion at the end of the eighteenth century, in the inaccurate and superficial version known as "Empire"; but as a matter of fact, although Le Roy's observations showed the French that the ruins of classical antiquity were not confined to Italy, they did very little to enlighten them as to the consummate technique of Greek architects. Gabriel, who was now sixty-five, was too old and much too busy to alter his manner of design, and I do not believe he ever had any intention of doing so, for the Trianon was not new, it was the culminating point of a manner of design which he had been steadily building up throughout his career, of which he had already given glimpses in the Place Royale and the École Militaire. The architecture of the Petit Trianon is purely French, as fine in its way as Greek architecture, but its way is a different way; the conditions under which Gabriel had to work and the ideals at which he aimed were altogether different from those of the architects of Pericles. If the

Comte de Fels had called the design of the Trianon Hellenistic instead of Hellenic, he might have been nearer the mark.

Gabriel retired from practice in 1775, tired out by the incessant demands of the Court ladies, the intrigues of the "Surintendant", and the impossibility of obtaining the money necessary for the schemes which he was instructed to make. Moreover the taste of the time was changing. Marie Antoinette brought with her from Vienna a predilection for the Baroque which the best French architects had rejected, the control of architecture was passing from the architects to the amateurs, the Academy of Architecture had itself played into the hands of the amateur by making one of the worst of them, the Comte de Caylus, an honorary member, and for nearly thirty-five years it had accepted his authority. Then came the discoveries of Pompeii and Herculaneum, the rise of Winckelmann and the archaeologists, and the final and finishing touch, the rise of the Romantics in literature. Gabriel must have felt that his time was past, and that it was better to spend his few remaining years in peace and quietness. His old enemy, Marigny, died in 1781, and in 1782 died M. Ange Jacques Gabriel, Knight, King's

Councillor, late Controller General of the buildings, gardens, arts and manufactures of France, first Architect of the King, Honorary Director of the Academy of Architecture, Honorary Member of the Academy of Painting and Sculpture, and Master of the Wardrobe of Madame. "After the Lord Mayor's coach comes the donkey-cart." The Master of the Wardrobe falls rather flat after all those other sonorous titles, but Gabriel was a great personage. There is a bust of him by Jean Baptiste Lemoyne, in the Louvre, in the free swaggering manner of that able sculptor. The head has a high, rather narrow forehead, and a heavy resolute jaw, the sort of face one would expect from a man of Gabriel's energetic, imperious and masterful character, a man who went his way undeterred by official menace and Court intrigue, loyal to his friends and just to his subordinates. But his memory remains, not because he was an important personage at the Court of Louis XV but because he was a great and distinguished artist, the last of the Old Guard in French architecture. He held a position in it very similar to that of Sir William Chambers in English architecture. Both men followed the tradition of their country, and carried it on to the highest point that it ever reached, but its days were numbered, the pedants and the archaeologists were at hand, to be followed by the revivalists who had abjured the inheritance of their fathers, and thought that living architecture was to be found in the graveyards of the past. So began that fatal divorce from the actual conditions of life which brought about the downfall of architecture and, after a hundred and fifty years of blundering experiment, has ended in the bankruptcy of the arts. To me at any rate as a lover of architecture and a student of its history, Ange Jacques Gabriel remains a great and admirable figure, one who never faltered in his faith that Architecture is indeed the Mistress art.

CHRISTOPHER WREN

SIR CHRISTOPHER WREN
From a bust by Edward Pearce, in the Ashmolean Museum at Oxford

CHRISTOPHER WREN

In the far-off days of Queen Victoria it used to be the custom to classify people as belonging to the upper, middle or lower classes. This foolish segregation has, I am glad to say, disappeared, though I do not know if classification by income is any better, but it is a fact that, with rather rare exceptions, great artists have risen from relatively humble origins, without advantages of birth, wealth or privilege. Palladio and Bernini were sons of rather obscure sculptors. Inigo Jones was the son of a draper. Mansart came of a building-contractor family. Gabriel, it is true, came from the upper ranks of the architectural hierarchy, but Christopher Wren almost alone was a gentleman—a scholar and an artist, less accomplished as a technician, but more attractive as a man, and endowed with greater powers of invention than any on my list.

Wren was born at East Knoyle in Wiltshire in 1631 or 1632, the son of a country Rector, who afterwards became Dean of

Windsor, and Registrar of the Order of the Garter. His uncle was Bishop of Ely, and remained a prisoner in the Tower for eighteen years, rather than abate his loyalty to the Throne. Wren was sent to Westminster School, and almost at once showed evidence of precocious ability. At the age of thirteen he wrote a dedication to his father in Latin verse of an astronomical invention. At the age of fifteen he translated a treatise on dialling into Latin, with the impressive title of *Sciotericon Catholicum*, and at the age of sixteen he wrote a treatise on trigonometry. Altogether an amazing youth.

In 1650 he entered as a gentleman commoner at Wadham College, and four years later was elected a Fellow of All Souls. No wonder that John Evelyn described him as "that miracle of youth and prodigious young scholar, Mr Christopher Wren". He was received on equal terms by the men who afterwards formed the Royal Society, such as Wilkins and Boyle. In 1657 he was appointed Gresham Professor of Astronomy, followed in 1661 by the Savilian Professorship of Astronomy at Oxford. The *Parentalia* gives a list of forty-four tracts on scientific subjects written by Wren, and by the age of thirty he was recognized as one of the first mathematicians of his time, and as a young man of most ingenious scientific invention. Yet so far there is not a trace of his having received any training in architecture, or paid any attention to the arts, or knowing anything whatever about them, except what he may have picked up from that rather priggish amateur, but extremely efficient backer, John Evelyn of Sayes Court, Deptford, who had published his translation of Fréart's *Parallels of Architecture* in 1663. Yet such was Wren's reputation at Oxford, and so strong was the claim of his family on the royal favour, that by what can only be described as the grossest of jobs, he was appointed Deputy Surveyor-General, with a promise of the reversion of the Surveyor-Generalship, and he succeeded to the latter post a few months later on the death of Sir John Denham. The appointment was the more shameless, because the reversion had already been promised to John Webb, the nephew, pupil and trusted assistant of Inigo Jones, an architect of ability and great experience steeped in the tradition of that great master, but Inigo Jones was already forgotten, and no doubt Charles II and his Court wanted to hear as little as possible of anything that reminded them of the tragedy of twenty years before. So in spite of his total lack of experience and technical training, Wren was instructed to examine and report on old St. Paul's and Windsor Castle, and to complete the designs made by Inigo Jones thirty years before for the Palace at Greenwich. It almost takes one's breath away to read in the *Parentalia* that in 1666 Wren, who so far had only designed Pembroke Chapel at Cambridge, an unimportant building, and the deplorable Sheldonian Theatre at Oxford, was appointed "Surveyor-General and Principal Architect for rebuilding the whole City, the Cathedral Church of St. Paul's, all the parochial churches, in number fifty-one, with other public structures". The whole affair of Wren's appointment is a standing example of discreditable jobbery, and of that disregard and even suspicion of trained opinion which appears to be ingrained in the English people, and yet, like other incidents in our extraordinary history, it was justified by success.

The Chapel of Pembroke College, Cambridge (1662), was Wren's earliest work, and it is the work of a young architect who knew very little of the technique of his art. He had at his disposal masons and carvers trained in the school of Inigo Jones, and Wren probably gave these men indications of what he wanted, relying both then, and indeed throughout his career, on their traditional skill, to carry out his instructions, for he had little of Inigo Jones' technical ability, and I have never found among the numerous drawings attributed to Wren any evidence to show that he was anything more than an indifferent draughtsman. It is also clear that when he designed the Chapel and also the Sheldonian, he was generally ignorant of the scholarship of architecture. The Corinthian pilasters on the front of the Chapel are some twelve diameters high. Nowadays the architects of Stockholm have taught us that they may be any number of diameters, but in those days the diameters of the orders were strictly laid down and invariably followed by trained architects, and I am convinced that Wren made his order twelve diameters because he thought it looked nice and did not know any better. So, too, the Sheldonian Theatre is about as bad as it can be. Wren contributed a well-designed queen-post roof, but on the outside the Sheldonian is just a great lump of a building, and as for the south front, with its slender Corinthian order below, and its atrocious Composite above, the misfits of its members, and its commonplace detail, it is perhaps the worst piece of architecture perpetrated in Oxford before the days of the Gothic revival and the dismal failures of Butterfield and Gilbert Scott. The grotesque terminal figures on the front to the Broad, are a clumsy recollection of the figures all round the forecourt of Vaux Le Vicomte, recently carried out from the designs of Le Vau. Wren never quite recovered the ground lost by his inadequate technical training, and it was this that gave its only justification to the contempt with which Wren was regarded by the English Palladians at the end of his career.

However, rightly or wrongly, Wren's appointment as Surveyor-General gave him his opportunity, and as time went on, he made magnificent use of his unrivalled good fortune. A position of such responsibility as that which he now held, might have frightened anyone with less confidence in his own ability, but Wren had no contemporary by whom to measure his own capacity. Inigo Jones was forgotten. Denham had not been an architect, John Webb was old, obscure and without powerful backing. With the exception of his brief visit to France, Wren never left the country, and appears to have known little of what was being done in Italy and elsewhere on the Continent. So, happy in the freedom of ignorance, but full of invention and resource, Wren sailed gaily on, and his own wonderful intelligence and power of assimilation enabled him to avoid disaster, till such time as he had really learnt his business. Of course, the first thing to do was to learn something more about architecture than could be learnt from Serlio and Scamozzi, and John Evelyn's conversation and translation of Fréart's *Parallels*. So in 1665, the year of the Plague, he went to Paris for six months to learn what he could from French architecture of the time. Le Vau had been superseded at the Louvre, and Bernini was vainly endeavouring to carry his design for the completion of the Palace in the face of the determined opposition of the French architects. Wren met Bernini but got little out of him. "The old reserved Italian", he says, "gave me but a few minutes' view. It was five little designs on paper for which he has received as many thousand pistoles." Wren mentions François Mansart, Le Vau and Le Pautre as leading French architects, but all of these men belonged to the older generation, and he does not appear to have met Perrault or any of the younger men who were soon to constitute the Academy of Architecture. He visited Fontainebleau and other famous houses, but there is no suggestion of anything approaching the close personal research which De l'Orme, Palladio and Inigo Jones had devoted to the study of old buildings and the technique of architecture. Instead of this, to use his own words, Wren brought back "all France on paper"; that is to say, by means of prints and engravings he took the short-cut to architecture which is now provided by the camera. The "paper" would have been the admirable engravings of the elder Marot, Israel Silvestre, Perelle, and the engraved designs of ornament produced with indefatigable regularity by Jean le Pautre, quite inadequate for the training of an architect, scarcely enough for an amateur. Wren's genius and the splendid attainment of his maturity sometimes blind us to the fact that he began as an amateur, and that throughout his career he was never quite certain of his technique. For example, the unsatisfactory treament of the angles of the octagon under the dome in the interior of St. Paul's, and the meaningless bays at the ends of the colonnade of the west front. So, too, the proportions of the garden front at Hampton Court are not satisfactory. The rusticated pedestals under the Corinthian columns of the stone centre-piece are too low and too abrupt, and the whole elevation seems to want lifting up on a plinth. In the Fountain Court Wren's treatment of the arcade is very unhappy. He wanted arches of a certain height, but in order to avoid bringing his windows down to the floor of the floor over, he used very shallow vaulting which appears half-way down the arches of the arcade. Here, as in the Library of Trinity College, Cambridge, the problem is not solved at all, and if it were not for its associations and magnificent siting, and its glorious composition with the garden, the Long Walk and the river—Hampton Court would not be the delightful and entirely lovable palace that it is.

Yet technique is not the last word in architecture; behind it all is what a man has to say and how he shapes at the problem before him—a man may have the whole paraphernalia of architectural detail, the orders of Classic, the machinery of Gothic at his fingers' ends, and yet may fail to impress us.

M

The essential point is whether he has any vision of his own, any fresh outlook on facts, any new version of their relations, whether he has a definite and original personality, for the personality of an architect is shown in his work quite as clearly as that of the painter and the sculptor in theirs. The architect's likes and dislikes, his ideals, his temperament and outlook are written on his work in ineffaceable letters. The mean and meticulous man will be mean and meticulous in his architecture, the small man will be small and the great man great, and it is this that gives its personal interest to architecture, an interest that will be swept into space if the present fashion of design survives, a manner that deliberately aims at wiping out the individual, and standardizing architecture by reducing it to the terms of a box of bricks.

So far I have suggested the unusual, and from the point of view of the art of architecture, unfavourable circumstances under which Wren began his great career. He started as an amateur, the Civil War had wiped out the standards of attainment built up by Inigo Jones, and so far as the arts were concerned, the state of affairs to some slight extent resembled the position left by the late war.

CHRISTOPHER WREN

Wren had to rely on himself, but it was just this that led to the realization of his astonishing genius. He was given a free hand and he had both the courage and the capacity to use it to the fullest possible extent. Wren was really the founder of modern town-planning. After the Great Fire of London, the City had to be rebuilt, and the plan which Wren drew up for the new city would, if it had been carried out, have made of London one of the most beautiful cities of the world. Hitherto London had been the usual incongruous ill-assorted collection of narrow streets and overhanging buildings left by the Middle Ages, and London did not possess the one great asset of Medieval towns, the wide open space, surrounded by buildings in which the citizens could assemble. Bernini, it is true, had designed the great Piazza of S. Peter's, and Lemercier had designed a complete new townlet, to house the officials and those in attendance on the great Cardinal, in his Château of Richelieu. But so far, the only deliberate attempt at town-planning on a far-reaching scale had been the great scheme for the reorganization of Paris known as the scheme of the "Porte et Place de France", prepared for Henri IV and never carried out.

Wren's scheme was on a much bigger and more comprehensive scale, for he was prepared to deal with the whole city, and he anticipated the essential ideas of the modern town-planner, axial planning, through communications, that organized relationship of street, square and buildings, which should govern the laying out of a city. This great conception of a city as a whole was lost sight of by his successors, till Ralph Allen employed John Wood and his son to reorganize Bath. Nash and Holland and others produced comprehensive schemes of layout in the days of the Regency, the one contribution to architecture of that deplorable period, but, with the three exceptions that I have noted, architects before Wren had confined their efforts to buildings complete with gardens and grounds as isolated units. It was Wren's great achievement that, given the opportunity of a new London, he treated it as a whole, with definite and considered relations between the various parts.

The area to be dealt with extended from the Tower of London at the south-east corner to the Temple Gardens at the south-west. The north boundary ran from Newgate to Aldersgate, Cripplegate, Bishopsgate and Aldgate back to the Tower, and all these points are marked on Wren's plan as actual gateways in the boundary wall. Wren's general idea was to form two main "Places"; that on the west was to be a circular "rond-point", about halfway up the hill between what is now Ludgate Circus and the Law Courts, with straight streets radiating from them east and west, north and south, and on the diagonal lines. The east "Place" was a large oblong, with semi-circular ends, with the Royal Exchange in the centre; a straight road ran from this to Ludgate, passing to the north of St. Paul's, and continuing with a slight slant to the north to the west "Place". From Ludgate another main road passing to the south of St. Paul's ran in a straight line due east ending in an open space north-west of the Tower, with two rond-points on the way, opening on to streets on the axis and diagonal lines. All the streets were straight, that is, there were to be no curved and irregular lines, and a terrace or quay was to run the whole length of the river from the Temple to the Tower. It was a magnificent scheme, far in advance of anything that had been done since the days of Rome. For the first time in modern architecture the attempt was made to link up important public buildings by broad straight streets. Wren saw at once that mere tinkering was foolishness, and that it was a question of a large idea or nothing. Unfortunately, his scheme was never even attempted. As happens invariably in old cities, vested interests were too strong for it. I encountered the same difficulty at Ypres. I had hoped to form a large Place to the east of the causeway from the Menin Gate and inside to open up a vista from the Cloth Hall to the gate. This could easily have been done by widening the main road some 10 feet but vested interests again were too strong. As for the Place it was lost in a multitude of estaminets and cafés.

The same splendid grasp of opportunity is shown in Wren's design for the completion of the Palace which Inigo Jones had designed for Charles I. The Queen's House, set far back from the river, remained as the centre-piece of a great court to be flanked by buildings on either side, with the fourth side open to the river. The Palace was finished by Wren's successors, but the river front is Wren's completion of Inigo Jones' design, and it is a masterly work, far more attractive than that monument of accomplished mediocrity, Versailles, where Jules Hardouin Mansart kept adding block to block till all semblance of fine composition was lost. Saint-Simon was justified when he said of Versailles: "La main d'œuvre est exquise en tout genre, l'ordonnance nulle". Mansart was a capable and unscrupulous thruster of great ability. No one can question the technical skill of Versailles, but does anybody like it? Does anybody regard that enormous building with anything more than a frigid admiration? It remains as unconvincing as Louis XIV himself, it represents not the great qualities of the French people, but their superficial and least attractive mannerisms. Greenwich and Hampton Court, compared with Versailles, are relatively modest buildings, but they are characteristic of all that is best in English architecture, its modesty and reticence, its freedom from affectation, its kindly humour and its unassuming dignity. Of all the royal palaces that I know, here and in other lands, these two are the most attractive, and the man to whose genius we owe them was Wren, the quiet, thoughtful, far-seeing man of infinite resource and invention, the one true Humanist in English architecture.

It was, perhaps, fortunate that Wren never went to Italy, and that his stay in France was a matter only of a few months, for it left him essentially English in his outlook. The only architecture with which he was really familiar was the architecture of his own country. The Civil War seems to have obliterated for a time the influence of Inigo Jones, and Wren reverted to some extent to an earlier tradition, for there is a definite Jacobean feeling in many of his towers and steeples, and in spite of frequent architectural solecisms, it is this combination of the wayward fancies of an earlier manner with the more solid classic to which he was feeling his way that gives so much of their charm to Wren's city churches.

I have already pointed out that Wren had in fact received little or no technical training, and this must always be borne in mind in any critical estimate of his work. Yet he advanced "per saltum", and one of the most astonishing things in Wren is the rapidity with which he picked up knowledge on every hand. He learnt his architecture on the scaffolding of his buildings, and from the consciousness, quickly realized, of the shortcomings of his own designs. His mind must have been extraordinarily alert, and that is the impression left by his portraits. Wren seems to have been ever on the watch, not for his own advancement, but for his improvement as an artist, and there could be no more signal instance of this than the history of the designs for St. Paul's Cathedral. When Inigo Jones began the rebuilding of old St. Paul's he started with a noble Roman portico at the west end, but through no fault of his own he got no further, and never reached the heart of the problem. In 1662 Wren was consulted about St. Paul's. At that time he knew very little about architecture, and he proposed to replace the great tower by a "dome or rotunda, and upon the cupola for outward ornament, a lantern with a spring top to rise proportionately". This was Wren's description, and it revealed at that time a complete inability to deal with the problem. Four years later the question was raised in earnest. Wren got out his design, and a horrible thing it was, as shown in the four drawings in the All Souls collection. The old Choir was to remain and over the crossing there was to be a dome with a lantern surmounted by a huge openwork pineapple 68 feet high. The Fire of London, September 2, 1666, saved Wren from attempting to realize this monstrous design. In 1668 Wren was instructed to clear the site and prepare designs for an entirely new Cathedral. With characteristic energy and complete lack of experience, Wren prepared several designs. Three only are of historical importance, the design which Wren preferred himself, and which was rejected owing to the obstinacy of the Duke of York and the timidity of the clergy, the Warrant design which was accepted by the authorities, and the design which was, in fact, carried out. The model of the rejected design is now in St. Paul's, and the plans, sections and elevations are in the All Souls Library. It consisted of a Greek cross on a square of 300 feet, with the four angles cut off on quadrant curves struck from the four angles of the square. Over the central space there was to be a dome 120 feet in diameter, 180 feet high above the floor, and constructed with outer and inner domes. The diameter of the Pantheon is 142 feet, that of S. Peter's at Rome 138 feet. It was a bold idea but there were liturgical objections; the clergy were afraid of it, and I think they were right. The exterior could not have been satisfactory, and Wren, still immature, was just feeling his way, but the idea of an inner and an outer dome with a lantern on the top of the outer dome was one step towards the final design.

The famous Warrant design was accepted in 1675, and this extraordinary freak has been a stumbling-block to all Wren's admirers, for the centre was to be covered by a dome 112 feet in diameter which stopped about halfway, and continued as a vertical drum 56 feet in diameter with an inner dome, and a false outer dome surmounted by a steeple in six storeys, like the steeple of St. Bride's, perhaps a vague reminiscence of the setbacks on the angle turrets of the south-west Tower of Ely. This has been explained as the result of worry and overwork, or as an attempt to please the Court. I regard it as the result of inadequate training, and of a taste which in spite of Wren's genius was never quite sure of itself. Anyhow, Wren managed to drop it as the work went slowly up, and by incessant thought and self-criticism arrived at the splendid result that was actually built.

Wren's advance, from the Warrant design to the design actually carried out, is one of the most astonishing things in the history of architecture. When one thinks of his later work, it is difficult to conceive how Wren could ever have produced such a grotesque design as the Warrant design, for he was not a young man at the time. Born in 1632, he was 43 years of age, but he was working single-handed. In the turmoil of the Civil War all standards in the arts had been obliterated. Inigo Jones and John Webb were forgotten. There were no colleagues of recognized ability to keep Wren in fear of what he was doing, and his taste was at the mercy of dangerous amateurs such as John Evelyn, and the heedless and ill-informed opinions of the favourites of Charles II. In the result, the authorities, finding themselves wholly ignorant of the subject, appear to have tossed up for the design to be carried out. The words of the Royal Warrant (1675) are significant: "Whereas among divers designs which have been presented to us, we have particularly pitched upon one, as well because we find it very proper, artificiall and useful, as because it was so ordered that it might be built and finished by parts". Charles II was too much occupied with his ladies to pay much attention to the matter, and the design approved by the Warrant was, in fact, one of the most preposterous designs ever made for a cathedral with its ill-designed portico, its commonplace flanking towers, terminating in candelabra, and the treatment of the central dome. All that can be said for it is that it contained the germs of the ultimate solution. The main ideas of the future St. Paul's were vaguely present in the design, the central dome, for example, and the motive of a portico with flanking towers in the west façade, but their expression was incredibly crude, and it was only Wren's freedom from the obsession of fixed ideas, his readiness to learn on every hand, and his quickness in advancing from point to point in design, that saved him from the fiasco of the Warrant design, and finally produced the glorious masterpiece of St. Paul's as we now have it. It is too often forgotten, and now more than ever, that architecture is a very difficult art, which requires a longer and more persistent apprenticeship than any of the arts. I am talking of the art of architecture, not of financial enterprise and the mechanized building that is now supposed to take its place. There is no short-cut to architecture, no such thing as brilliant improvisation, no escaping the incessant critical analysis of one's own work if one is to advance to higher things. Wren was great enough to realize his own shortcomings, and he was ever on the watch to correct them. His case, if ever there was one, bears witness to the soundness of the "gymnastic" view of education, the view, that is, that it is not the ideal of education to take a boy young and cram his memory with quantities of specialized facts. The only real education is that which trains the mind, so that when the boy enters on the calling of his life, he can attack his specialized studies with a trained intelligence. To make a boy specialize at sixteen is like throwing a child into the water before he can swim, and the chances are that he will never come to the top again. Few people possess the extraordinary endowments of Christopher Wren, but even Wren could not have mastered his art with the rapidity that he did had he not received a thorough education on the broadest lines possible at that time.

To the serious architect, who regards architecture not only as a profession, but as a great and vital art, there are two problems still unsettled, the training of architects and the manner of expression. In spite of repeated experiments, we are still uncertain how to train our students and how to express ourselves. For the old system of apprenticeship we have substituted schools. The old system had its faults, but it at least brought the pupil into touch with actual buildings and the practice of architecture. Our schools produce young architects full of theories and familiar with ideal palaces, municipal buildings, town halls and casinos, but ignorant of what has been done in the past, and instead of unravelling the knot of architecture, they have cut it in two and left the loose ends lying on the ground. Our students are set to face difficult problems before they have any standard of critical judgment. Where we are wrong is, I believe, in closing down general education too soon, and forcing a specialized training too early, and it is impossible to catch up this initial defect. Wren began very late, too late in fact, but he possessed an admirably equipped intellectual machine, and was able to race through stages that would have cost years of struggle to minds less thoroughly disciplined.

It will be said that Wren was a man of genius and therefore exceptional, and that for the average man a specialized technical training, begun at an early date, is essential, but here we reach another fallacy, namely, that the average man, that is the man with no particular bent or ability, can become a good architect if he is sufficiently trained. To this I would say that the good architect, and by him I mean not the business man or the building policeman, but the artist in building, is not an average man at all, but as rare and exceptional as the poet, the painter, the musician and the sculptor. It is one of the mistakes of our system of State-aided art training that it assumes that given the technical training, anybody can become an artist. Over 2000 years ago Plato pointed out that it was futile for the mere technician to attempt to enter the palace of art: "ὃς δ' ἄνευ μανίας Μουσῶν ἐπὶ ποιητικὰς θύρας ἀφίκηται, πεισθεὶς ὡς ἄρα ἐκ τέχνης ἱκανὸς ποιητὴς ἐσόμενος, ἀτελὴς αὐτός" (Plato, *Phædrus* 245 A). "He who without the fine frenzy of the Muses approaches the doors of creative art, believing that merely technical ability will make him an artist, will fail of his purpose." Behind all art worth considering there must be enthusiasm for high ideals as well as technical ability. Yet our educational authorities in their anxiety to please the Teachers' Union persist in their extravagant systems of State-aided art training, and the results are seen in the hopeless overstocking of the market by incompetent performers in all the arts. It may be a generous idea to cast the net wide in the hope of catching a Triton among the minnows, but this is unskilful fishing. History shows that the Triton in the arts will push his way through now as he has always done, and it is no use providing people with a costly apparatus, unless they have the ability to profit by it.

Wren's work is so familiar and so generally appreciated that it needs no panegyric, but I would suggest that he was a true modernist in the right sense, in that he met each problem that presented itself squarely on its merits, and made no attempt to twist it and turn it to suit a formula or a fashion. Moreover he was true to the tradition of his country, for no man's work is more characteristically English than Wren's in its charm and kindliness, and, in spite of occasional technical shortcomings, its simple dignity. The men who succeeded him, Lord Burlington and his obsequious clique of architects, such as Kent and Colen Campbell, affected to despise Wren's work because it did not conform to the practice of the Ancients as laid down by Andrea Palladio. To Wren such pedantry would have seemed foolish, and if he erred at all it was in the opposite direction. In all his work he showed the strong practical sense and freedom from affectation which has always been one of the best traditions of the English people.

In 1718 at the age of eighty-six, Wren was superseded in the post of Surveyor-General owing to a disgraceful intrigue. Wren met the situation with the quiet dignity which had characterized the whole of his career. His reply to the Commission of Inquiry ended with the words: "As I am dismissed having worn out by God's mercy a long life in the Royal service, and having made some figure in the world, I hope it will be allowed me to die in peace". On February 25, 1723, Wren passed away in his sleep "cheerful in solitude, and as well pleased to die in the shade as in the light", as his son says, referring to the neglect of his latter years.

In his inexhaustible resource, his high outlook and his freedom from the egotism and personal ambition that do so easily beset us, Wren remains the nearest approach that I know to the ideal architect. Technical shortcomings, on which his work is sometimes open to criticism, are insignificant in comparison with his greatness both as an architect and as a man. His large conception of his art, his invention and ability both in plan and construction, are far above the level of the merely learned technician, and behind it all was Wren himself, the gentleman and the scholar, wise, humorous and equable, a delightful companion, an artist above self-seeking and advertisement. "Nec te venditas popello, Robertelle" ("Nor do you play to the gallery"), as was said of the late Lord Roberts. One does not think of Wren as one does of the younger Mansart, thrusting his way to the front, elbowing his rivals out of his path, betraying his friends, arriving at a Marquisate with salaries and perquisites amounting to not less than £20,000 a year, and dying only just in time to escape detection and complete disgrace. Wren had for years carried out his duties as Surveyor-General on a salary of £300 a year, not always paid him in full. He ended his days in retirement and comparative neglect, pushed out of office by the intrigues of knaves and charlatans, but in his lifetime he enjoyed the esteem and affection of some of the best men of his time. He left behind him, perhaps, the finest reputation ever won by any artist of this country, and no one has ever seriously questioned the justice of that proud epitaph in St. Paul's Cathedral: "Si monumentum requiris, circumspice".

In these critical studies I have endeavoured to call attention to six famous men, who differed in character, in their ideals and in their outlook on life, but each of whom did work worthy of remembrance, and in the world of art, as in the kingdom of heaven, there are many mansions. The danger nowadays is that artists such as these are almost forgotten in the rush of modern life. We are still suffering from the aftermath of the war, the break-up of tradition and the loss of all standards of value. The fashion flits from one sensation to another, restless, sterile, and impatient, and for the moment it is the cult of ugliness that holds the field in Literature, Music and the Arts, but I do not believe that this morbid development will be permanent. Deep down in our people there is an abiding sense of the continuity of things, which will in due course assert itself and will not tolerate the attempt to break utterly with the past. We of the present have to set our face forward, but only fools or madmen would ignore the experience of those who have gone before.

AUTHORITIES

Palladio

Temanza, Tommaso, *Vite dei più celebri Architecti, scultori Veneziani*, 284-408. Venice, 1778.
Quattro Libri dell' Architectura di Andrea Palladio. Venice, 1570.
Milizia, *Lives of Celebrated Architects*, translated by Mrs Edward Cresy, ii. 30-46. London, 1826.
The Architecture of A. Palladio, revised by Giacomo Leoni, translated from the Italian. London, 1721. 2 vols.
Banister Fletcher, *Andrea Palladio, his Life and Works*. London, 1902.
Quatremère de Quincy, *Histoire de la vie et des ouvrages des plus célèbres Architectes*, ii. 1-28. Paris, 1830.

Bernini

Baldinucci, Filippo, *Vita del Cavaliere Gio. Lorenzo Bernini*. Florence, 1682.
Fraschetti, Stanislas, *Il Bernini*. Milan, 1900.
Quatremère de Quincy, *op. cit.* ii. 155-186.
Milizia, *op. cit.* ii. 203-228.

Inigo Jones

Cunningham, Peter, *Inigo Jones*, London, 1848.
Campbell, Colen, *Vitruvius Britannicus*, ii. 2-19, i. 12-13 (1717).

Kent, W., *Inigo Jones, Architecture*, 1727.
Vardy, J., *Some Designs of Inigo Jones*, 1744.
Ware, Isaac, *Designs of Inigo Jones*, 1757.
The Designs of Inigo Jones. Published by W. Kent; printed in 1835 by Nichols, London.
Blomfield, Reginald, *A History of Renaissance Architecture in England*, i. 96-122 (1897, London).
Quatremère de Quincy, *op. cit.* ii. 129-141.
Walpole, Horace, *Anecdotes of Painting*, ii. 52-66.
Belcher, T., and Macartney, M., *Later Renaissance. Architecture in England*. London, 1901.

Mansart

Perrault, Charles, *Receuil des hommes illustres qui ont paru en France*, Paris, 1698.
Blondel, Jacques François, *Cours d'Architecture*, vi. 495-496. Paris, 1777. *Architecture française*. Paris, 1752.
Nicolle, Henri, *Le Château de Maisons*, Paris, 1858.
Anciens Hôtels de Paris, l'Hôtel d'Aumont, Paris, 1910.
Blomfield, Reginald, *A History of French Architecture*, 1494–1661, ii. 107-135. London, 1911.
Bauchal, Charles, *Nouveau Dictionnaire des Architectes français*. Paris, 1887.
Milizia, *op. cit.* ii. 177-179.

Gabriel

Fels, Comte Edmund de, *Ange Jacques Gabriel*, Paris, 1912.
Wilson and Arnott, *The Petit Trianon*. Versailles— London, 1907.

AUTHORITIES

Patte, Pierre, *Monuments érigés en France à la gloire de Louis XV*, Paris, 1765.
Cazes, E., *Le Château de Versailles*. Versailles, 1910.
Blomfield, Reginald, *A History of French Architecture*, 1661-1774, ii. 121-133. London, 1921.
Quatremère de Quincy, *op. cit.* ii. 310-320.

WREN

Wren, Stephen, *Parentalia*. London, 1750.
Elmes, James, *Memoirs of the Life and Works of Sir Christopher Wren*. 1823.
Elmes, James, *Life of Sir Christopher Wren and his Times*. London, 1852.
Longman, *A History of the Three Cathedrals dedicated to St. Paul*. 1873.
Milman, Lena, *Sir Christopher Wren*. 1908.
Loftie, W. J., *Inigo Jones and Wren*. 1893.
Law, Ernest, *A History of Hampton Court*. 1885-1891.
Blomfield, Reginald, *A History of Renaissance Architecture in England*, i. 148-186 (1897).
The Publications of the Wren Society.
Birch, George, *London Churches of the 17th and 18th Centuries*. 1896.
Belcher and Macartney, *Later Renaissance Architecture in England*. 1901.

INDEX

Academy of Architecture, French, 132, 137, 138, 139, 140, 146-147, 153, 166
Academy of Painting, French, 132
Academy of Sculpture, French, 132
Alberti, Leon Battista, 19, 20, 22, 23, 74
Alexander VII, Pope, 54, 55, 62
Algardi, Alessandro, 63
Algarotti, Francesco, 28
Allen, Ralph, 170
Almerigo, Paolo, 14
Amiens Cathedral, 103
Anet, De l'Orme's chapel at, 120
Angaranno, Count, 17
Anne of Austria, 120, 122
Antin, Duc d', 138
Antiquities of Rome, Ligori's, 19
Antiquities of Rome, Palladio's, 10
Architects, education of, 179-183
Architectura, Palladio's, 8, 10, 12, 13, 16-21, 23, 24, 78
Argouge, Hôtel d', 117
Artois, Comte d', 114
Arundel, Earl of, 86
Ashburnham House, 94, 112
Audley End, 73

Bacon, Francis, 7
Baldinucci, Filippo, 46

Balleroy, Normandy, 109-110, 111
Banque de France, 109
Baratta, Giovanni, 51
Barbaro, Daniele, 19, 28, 74
Barberini, Cardinal Maffeo, 38, 43, 46. *See also* Urban VIII
Barberini family, the, 45, 48, 49
Baroque architecture, 16, 64, 65, 78, 138, 153
Basing House, Hampshire, 92
Bath, Wood's re-planning of, 170
Berni, Château of, 110, 116
Bernini, Lorenzo, 16, 36-66, 87, 105, 117, 123, 124-125, 137, 159, 165, 169
Bernini, Paolo, 62
Bernini, Pietro, 37
Bibiena brothers, the, 94
Blois, Château of, 110-113, 136, 148
Blondel, François, 105, 117, 121, 125-126
Bloome, Hans, 74
Bodley's Tower, Oxford, 73
Bolgi, Andrea, 45
Bolsover, 73, 74
Bordeaux, 136
Borghese, Cardinal Scipio, 39, 41, 64
Borghese Gallery, Rome, 38
Borromini, Francesco, 16, 36, 47, 49-50, 63, 64, 87

191

Bouchardon, Edme, 139
Boyle, Robert, 160
Bramante, Donato, 23
Bray, Sir Reginald, 75
Brosse, Jacques de, 107
Brosse, Salomon de, 107
Browne, Sir Thomas, 7
Brunelleschi, Filippo, 23, 69
Buckingham Palace, 141
Budleigh, Somerset, 78
Bullant, Jean, 74, 107, 108
Buonarelli, Costanza, 47
Burlington, Lord, 23, 80, 88, 183
Bussy-Rabutin Tanlay, Burgundy, 107
Butterfield, William, 164

Caliari, Paolo (Veronese), 22, 28
Calza, Company of the, 81
Campbell, Colen, 23, 88, 183
Cany Banville, Château of, 110
Caprarola, 37
Carcassonne, 116
Carnavalet, Hôtel, 117
Casa del Diavolo, Vicenza, 11
Cateneo, Pietro, 28
Caux, Solomon de, 86
Caylus, Comte de, 153
Chambers, Sir William, 30, 70, 154
Chambord, 17
Chambray, M. de, 59. See also Fréart
Champs-Élysées, the, 140, 141
Charles I, 23, 48, 82, 85, 88, 89, 90, 93
Charles II, 92, 93, 161, 178
Chatsworth, 95
Cheverney, 144
Chevreuse, Mme de, 117

Chigi, Fabio, 54. See also Alexander VII, Pope
Christian IV (of Denmark), 79, 80, 85
Christina of Sweden, 46, 55-56, 64
Clarendon, Lord, 92
Cloth Hall, Ypres, 172
Colbert, Jean-Baptiste, 58, 59, 122, 123, 131-133, 135
Coleshill, Berkshire, 93
Compiègne, 147, 150
Compton Wynyates, 71
"Congregazione della Fabrica di San Pietro", the, 50
Copenhagen Exchange, 79
Cortona, Pietro da, 59
Cotte, Robert de, 133, 140
Cotte, de, family of, 135
Crequi, Duc de, 59
Cromwell, Oliver, 73, 92, 93

Danvers, Lord, 86
Dauboeuf, Château of, 110
Davenant, Sir William, 85
Daviler, 133
De Lisle, Marie, 136
De l'Orme, Philibert, 18, 74, 87, 89, 90, 107, 108, 120, 166
De Re Aedificatoria, Alberti's, 19
De Rubeis, 120
De Vries, 73, 74
Denham, Sir John, 161, 164
Desgodetz, 11, 133, 137
Devonshire, Duke of, 95
Dieterlin, Wendel, 73, 74
Dorbay family, the, 135
Du Barri, Mme, 134, 145, 149, 150, 151
Du Cerceau family, the, 107, 135

INDEX

Du Gers, or Du Jars, Commandeur, 116-117
Du Perac, Etienne, 19
Duverney, Paris, 143, 145

East Knoyle, Wiltshire, 159
École Militaire, Paris, 142, 143-144, 145-146, 152
Elizabethan architecture, 73
Ely Cathedral, 177
"Empire" period, 152
English architecture, 70-77, 96, 97, 98, 103, 173, 183
Este, Francesco, Duke of, 64
Evelyn, John, 160, 161, 165, 178

Faithorne, William, 92
Fannelli, 51
Fauno, 19
Fels, Comte de, 151-152, 153
Ferrata, Ercole, 54
Feuillants, Church of the (Paris), 109, 118
Fiammingo, Il, 45, 53
Florence, Academy of, 28
Florence Museum, 47
Fontainebleau, 107, 145, 150, 166
Fontana, Domenico, 87
Footscray, Kent, 14
Ford Abbey, Wiltshire, 93
Fountains, Bernini's, 51-54
Fouquet, Nicolas, 132
François I, 19, 20, 72, 106, 108, 110, 112, 144
Fraschetti, Signor, 37, 41, 42
Fréart, Roland, 59, 161, 165
Frederiksborg, Castle of, 79, 80
French Academy, Rome, 132, 138
French architecture, 14, 103, 126, 131, 154, 165-166

Fulvio, 19
Functionalism, 15

Gabriel, Ange Jacques, 104, 135, 137-155
Gabriel, Jacques, 135-136
Gabriel, Jacques Jules, 136, 137
Gabriel family, the, 133, 135-137
Galanti, Angelica, 37
Garde-Meuble, Paris, 141
Gautier, Germain, 106
Giocondo, Fra, 19, 20, 23, 74
Gothic revival, 5, 164
Goujon, Jean, 58, 117
Greek architecture, 10, 13, 17, 151-153
Greek sculpture, 41, 42
Greenwich Hospital, 92
Greenwich Palace, 92, 162, 172, 173
Gustavus Adolphus, 55

Haddon Hall, 71
Hampton Court, 26, 167, 173
Hardouin, Jules. *See* Mansart, J. H.
Hardouin family, the, 135
Hatfield, 73
Henri IV, 106, 107, 109, 131, 169
Henrietta, Queen, 48, 50
Henry, Prince of Wales, 86
Henry VII Chapel, 75
Henry VIII, 72, 73
Hittorf, Jacques-Ignace, 142
Holland, Henry, 170
Hollar, Wenceslaus, 92
Hommes Illustres, Perrault's, 105, 122
"House of Fame", Inigo Jones', 82-84

Hypnerotomachia Polyphili, 54
Hyrcanus, King of Jerusalem, 81

Innocent X, Pope, 49, 50, 51, 54

James I, 70, 80, 81, 82, 85, 88, 89
John of Padua, 75
Jones, Inigo, 23, 70-71, 76, 77-97, 98, 112, 117, 124, 125, 126, 159, 161, 162, 163, 164, 166, 168, 172, 174, 175, 178
Jonson, Ben, 77-78, 81, 82, 83, 84, 85-86, 87, 91, 95, 96, 97

Kent, William, 14, 23, 88, 183
Kirby, Northants, 93

La Hire, Laurent de, 137
La Motte, Catherine de, 138
La Rochelle Cathedral, 136
Labacco, 19, 87
Lafitte, Jacques, 115
Lannes, Marshal, 115
Laud, Archbishop, 91
Law, John, 134
Law Courts, London, 171
Le Duc, 121
Le Muet, Pierre, 107, 121
Le Pautre, Jean, 165, 166
Le Roy, 152
Le Vau, Louis, 58, 123, 164, 165
Lemercier, Jacques, 107, 108, 118, 121, 169
Lemoyne, Jean, 154
Leoni, 8, 22, 95
Leto, Pomponius, 19
Licinio, Bernardino, 9
Ligori, Pyrrho, 19

Lincoln's Inn Fields, 88, 92
Lindsay House, Lincoln's Inn Fields, 92
London, Wren's scheme for the re-planning of; 169-173
Longeuil, René de, 113
Longeuil, de, family of, 114
Longhi, Martino, 50
Longleat, Wilts, 75
Lorges, Maréchal de, 137
Louis XIII, 48, 108, 109, 110, 149
Louis XIV, 10, 58, 59, 61, 62, 64, 106, 121, 125, 134, 149, 173
Louis XV, 122, 140, 142, 149, 150, 151, 154
Louis XVI, 114, 151
Louvre, the, 58, 60-61, 106, 108, 120, 122, 123, 133, 141, 150, 154, 165
Luxembourg, the, Paris, 108

Madeleine, La, Paris, 140
Maderno, Carlo, 45, 49
Maison Carrée, Nîmes, 17, 18
Maisons, Château of, 110, 113-116
Mansarade, 122
Mansart, Absalom, 106
Mansart, François, 103-106, 108-127, 131, 136, 137, 138, 144, 149, 165
Mansart, J. H., 105, 106, 133, 136, 137, 138, 148, 149, 172-173, 185
Mansart, Jehan, 106
Mansart, Pierre, 106
Mansart family, the, 106, 135, 136
Mantegna, Andrea, 26
Marie Antoinette, 151, 153
Marigny, Marquis de, 140, 145, 146-147, 148, 153

INDEX

Marliani, 19
Marot (the elder), 166
Marot (the younger), 116
Masque of Blackness, Jonson's, 81, 85
Masque of Queens, Jonson's, 82
Masques, 81-85, 95, 96
Matteo, 47
Mazarin, Cardinal, 59, 131, 132
Medicis, Marie de, 107
Meissonnier, 138
Menars, Château of, 148
Menin Gate, Ypres, 172
Mereworth, Kent, 14
Michael Angelo, 24, 36, 37, 40, 42, 66, 120
Milizia, Francesco, 48
Mirabel Gardens, Salzburg, 40
Miromesnil, Château of, 110
Mochi, Francesco, 45, 46
Modernism, 3-7, 15, 29, 30-31, 97-99, 118, 186
Monaldeschi, Jean, 55
Montebello, Duc de, 115
Montebello, Mme de, 115
Museo Civico, Vicenza, 21

Naples, 9, 37, 38, 105
Nash, John, 170
Neo-classic architecture, 17, 23, 69, 70, 78, 90, 96, 107, 108, 111, 119, 121, 151
Nîmes, 17, 18
Nonesuch, palace of, 72-73

Opera House, Versailles, 148-149
Oppenord, Gilles, 126, 138
Orders of architecture, the, 6, 18, 21, 73-74, 108, 109, 163

Orleans, Duc d', 110, 111
Oxford, 73, 161, 162

Paestum, 9, 17
Palace of the Propaganda, Rome, 50
Palais Mazarin, Paris, 122
Palazzo Albergati, Bologna, 12, 26
Palazzo Thiene, Vicenza, 90
Palladio, Andrea, 8-31, 56, 69, 74, 78, 79, 81, 82, 86, 87, 90, 95, 159, 166, 183
Palladio, Pietro, 8
Pamphili, Olimpia, 50, 51
Pamphili family, the, 49
Pantheon, Rome, 44, 176
Parallels of Architecture, Fréart's, 59, 161, 165
Parentalia, 161, 162
Paul III, Pope, 10
Paul V, Pope, 38
Pembroke, Earl of, 86
Pembroke Chapel, Cambridge, 162, 163
Perelle, 110, 113, 116, 166
Perrault, Charles, 59, 105, 122, 124
Perrault, Claude, 124, 141, 166
Perronet, Jean-Rodolphe, 141
Peruzzi, Baldassare, 12, 24, 26, 28, 74, 81, 127
Petit Trianon, Versailles, 14, 142, 145, 150-153
Piazza Agonale, Rome, 51, 53
Piazza del Popolo, Rome, Church of the, 50
Piazza della Minerva, Rome, 54
Piazza di S. Pietro, Rome, 56-58

Piazza Navona, Rome, 51, 53
Pierrefonds, Château of, 116
Place de France, Paris, 108
Place de la Bourse, Bordeaux, 136
Place de la Concorde, Paris, 139-142
Place Louis XV, Paris, 139-142
Place Royale, Bordeaux, 136
Place Royale, Paris, 108, 146, 152
Plato, 182
Pompadour, Mme de, 134, 140, 142, 143, 146, 148, 149, 150
Pordenone, 9
Porissimi, 51
Porta del Popolo, Rome, 55
"Porte et Place de France", Paris, 108, 169
Poussin, Gaspar, 77
Primaticcio, Francesco, 107, 150

Queen's House, Greenwich, 88, 92, 94, 112, 172

Raggi, Antonio, 51
Rainaldi, Carlo, 50, 59, 62
Rambouillet, Château of, 145
Raphael, 23, 28
Raynham, Norfolk, 93
Redentore, Il, Venice, 13, 15
Religio Medici, Browne's, 7
Renaissance, the, 9, 17, 24, 27, 36-37, 54, 83
Rennes, Hôtel de Ville, 136, 139
Revivalism, 5-6, 118, 155
Richelieu, Cardinal, 47-48, 107, 108, 110, 111, 117, 131, 169
Richelieu, Château, 107, 169

Roberts, Lord, 185
Robinson, actor, 92
Romano, Giulio, 28
Rosa, Salvator, 63
Rosenborg Palace, Copenhagen, 79
Rosso, Il, 107
Rouen town-hall, 135
Royal Exchange, 171
Royal Society, 160
Royal Staff of Architects, 134
Royal Warrant (1675), the, 178
Rue Royale, Paris, 140, 141

Sacchi, Andrea, 63
S. Agnese, Rome, 50
S. Agostino, Rome, 43
S. Andrea al Quirinale, Rome, 58
S. Angelo, Castle of, Rome, 43, 44, 62
St. Bennet, Paul's Wharf, 93
St. Bride's, London, 177
St. Denis, chapel of the Valois, 120
S. Giorgio, Venice, 13, 15, 28
St. Gregory, London, 92
S. John Lateran, Rome, 50
S. John of the Florentines, Rome, 120
S. Lucia, Venice, 28
S. Maria Maggiore, Rome, 37, 62
Ste. Marie, Paris, 118-119, 120
St. Paul's, Covent Garden, 91
St. Paul's Cathedral, 91, 162, 166-167, 171, 175-179, 185
S. Peter's, Rome, 10, 43, 44, 45, 49, 50, 52, 53, 56, 57, 62, 169, 176
S. Petronio, Bologna, 28
Santo Spirito, Florence, 69

INDEX

Saint-Simon, 124, 173
Sala della Ragione, Vicenza, 11, 56
Sala Ducale, Vatican, 58
Salmacida Spolia, Davenant's, 85
San Gallo, Antonio da (the elder), 24
San Gallo, Antonio da (the younger), 24
San Gallo, Giuliano da, 23
Sanmichele, Michele, 24
Sansovino, Giacomo, 23
Sansovino, Jacopo, 28
Sayes Court, Deptford, 161
Scala Regia, Vatican, 58
Scamozzi, Vincenzo, 87, 165
Sciotericon Catholicum, Wren's, 160
Scott, Sir Gilbert, 164
Serlio, Sebastian, 19, 20, 25, 74, 87, 107, 165
Sheldonian Theatre, Oxford, 162, 163-164
Silvestre, Israel, 166
Smithson, Huntingdon, 74
Smithson, Robert, 74
Smithson family, the, 75
Somerset House, 92
Stage innovations, 81-82, 94-95, 96
Stahlman, G. F., 80
Star Chamber, Inigo Jones', 88
Stone, Nicholas (the elder), 91, 92
Stonehenge Restored, Inigo Jones', 78
Street, G. E., 5

Tale of a Tub, Jonson's, 78
Temanza, Tommaso, 27
Temple of Nemausus, Nîmes, 17, 18
Temple of Neptune, Paestum, 10
Terribilia, 28
Tezio, Caterina, 48
Thomas, M., 115
Thorpe, John, 75
Titian, 28
Toulouse, Hôtel de Paris, 109
Tournchem, — de, 145
Town-planning, 169-170
Traditionalism, 5-8, 118
Trinity College Library, Cambridge, 167
Trissino, Gian Giorgio, 9
Tuileries, Paris, 89, 106, 139, 140

Urban VIII, Pope, 38, 43, 44, 45, 46, 47, 49; monument, 62
Urbis Romae Topographia, Marliani's, 19

Val de Grace, 110, 120
Vandieres, de, 140
Vandyck, 48, 93
Vasari, Giorgio, 28
Vatican, the, 45, 56, 57, 58
Vaux Le Vicomte, 164
Venice, 11, 13, 15, 19, 25, 27, 28, 79, 81, 87
Veronese, 22, 28
Versailles, Palace of, 64, 105, 124, 133, 139, 145, 148-149, 150, 172, 173; Petit Trianon, 14, 142, 145, 150-153
Vicenza, 8, 9, 11, 12, 13, 14, 15, 18, 21, 25, 26, 56, 79, 81, 82, 86, 90
Vignola, 21, 24, 25, 28, 37, 69, 74, 87
Villa Capra or Almerigo, 14

Villa Malcontenta, 14
Villas, Palladio's, 13, 14, 15, 25, 27
Vitruvius, 11, 16, 17, 19, 20, 74, 94
Vitruvius Britannicus, Campbell's, 88

Wailly, de, 146, 147
Warrant design, the, 176, 177
Watergate, York House, the, 91
Webb, John, 79, 93, 94, 161, 164, 178

Whitehall, Banqueting-House at, 88-90, 94
Wilkins, John, 160
Wilton, Wilts, 93, 94
Wollaton, 73, 74
Wood, Anthony, 81
Wood, John, 170
Wren, Sir Christopher, 23, 26, 70, 92, 95, 159-181, 183-185

York House, 91
Ypres, 172

Zucchero, Federigo, 28

THE END

www.ingramcontent.com/pod-product-compliance
Lightning Source LLC
Chambersburg PA
CBHW020329170426
43200CB00006B/323